Time Management

SELF-DEVELOPMENT FOR MANAGERS
A major series of workbooks for managers edited by Jane Cranwell-Ward.

This series presents a selection of books in workbook format, on a range of key management issues and skills. The books are designed to provide practising managers with the basis for self-development across a wide range of industries and occupations.

Each book relates to other books in the series to provide a coherent new approach to self-development for managers. Closely based on the latest management training initiatives, the books are designed to complement management development programmes, in-house company training, and the management qualification programmes such as CMS, DMS, MBA and professional qualification programmes.

Other books in the series:

Thriving on Stress
Jane Cranwell-Ward

Accounting for Managers
Roger Oldcorn

Managing Change
Colin Carnall

Developing Assertiveness
Anni Townend

Effective Problem Solving
Dave Francis

The Self-reliant Manager
Chris Bones

Step-by-step Competitive Strategy
Dave Francis

Effective Marketing
Geoffrey Randall

Improving Environmental Performance
Suzanne Pollack

Developing the Manager as a Helper
John Hayes

The New Flexi-manager
David Birchall

Jane Cranwell-Ward is at Henley Management College. She is the author of *Managing Stress* (Pan, 1986).

Time Management

Chris Croft

Senior Lecturer in Management
Bournemouth Business School

INTERNATIONAL THOMSON BUSINESS PRESS
I ⒯ P An International Thomson Publishing Company

London • Bonn • Boston • Johannesburg • Madrid • Melbourne • Mexico City • New York • Paris
Singapore • Tokyo • Toronto • Albany, NY • Belmont, CA • Cincinnati, OH • Detroit, MI

To my wife Sally, who is in box 1 (see chapter 3).
Additional thanks to Louise, Miles and Marmite for teaching me about Quality of Life, Mike Jinks for introducing me to personality drivers, my mother Brit for chapter 4, and the Blue Nile and Miles Davis for creative work atmosphere.

Time Management

Copyright © 1996 Chris Croft

First published 1996 by International Thomson Business Press

I ⓉP   A division of International Thomson Publishing Inc.
The ITP logo is a trademark under licence

British Library Cataloguing-in-Publication Data
A catalogue record for this book is available from the British Library

First edition 1996

Typeset in Times by Lisa Williams
Printed in the UK by Biddles Ltd, Guildford and King's Lynn

ISBN 0–415–13566–4

International Thomson Business Press
Berkshire House
168–173 High Holborn
London WC1V 7AA
UK

International Thomson Business Press
20 Park Plaza
14th Floor
Boston MA 02116
USA

Contents

WASTED & USEFUL LIVES

— Series editor's preface

Most managers today are experiencing increased workloads and reduced resources to achieve challenging business goals. Faced with this scenario the skills associated with time management have grown in importance.

Time Management has been written for the manager who is keen to achieve the most out of life. In line with the Self-development for Managers Series the book helps the reader develop this important skill. Checklists are used to help the reader identify his or her level of skill and identify issues to be addressed. Readers will be better able to establish both business and life goals and work more effectively to achieve results. The book investigates some of the attitudes which might need to be changed if people are to achieve their vision of the future.

Although the book has been written primarily for managers it is likely to appeal to a wider audience. It stresses the importance of a balanced life and of achieving results at home as well as at work. The book includes a range of useful tips to improve time management which can be applied to a range of situations.

A book on Time Management had always been planned for the Self-development for Managers Series. We had reviewed several proposals before Chris Croft was selected. Chris is certainly one of the authors who can set an example in his subject area. He submitted his manuscript ahead of time and I have learned some useful hints on achieving results. I constantly visualize my tidy desk and am starting to win the paperwork battle!

Time Management will complement the other books in the series well, in particular *Thriving on Stress* and *Developing Assertiveness*. Apart from books written to help develop personal skills the Self-development for Managers Series also includes a range of titles written to develop strategic capability.

Jane Cranwell-Ward
Series Editor

— *Acknowledgements*

Copyright in the cartoon on pp. vi is held by Penguin USA. Permission to reproduce the material has been requested.

— *Introduction*

WHY SHOULD YOU READ THIS BOOK?

The objective of this book is to help you to think about your life at the moment, and to help you to improve it. This is a book about success. Success does not necessarily mean money or ambition, but can be success on *your* terms. It could mean:

- quality of life
- peace of mind
- having as much fun as possible
- experiencing better personal relationships with others
- being really good at just one thing, either at work or outside work.

In all of the above, time management is vitally important. It is perhaps the single biggest ingredient in whether you achieve a current lifestyle that you enjoy and a future life with which you will be satisfied. I would like to illustrate this with four types of holiday:

FOUR FAILED HOLIDAYS

1	We had a terrible journey, but it was good when we arrived.
2	The journey was OK, but we were disappointed in the destination when we arrived.
3	The travel was very efficient and fast, but we went round in a circle and ended up where we started.
4	The journey was quite pleasant, but we had no destination so we didn't arrive anywhere special.

The first two are probably familiar to you. The third type may not be, but if you have ever had a 'Been there, done that' tour of a country you may have experienced it. The fourth one may seem incredible, hardly qualifying as a holiday at all: how can anyone go on holiday without a destination? Yet in terms of how we live our *lives*, the fourth type is the commonest.

The four types of holiday can all be equated with approaches to living our lives:

---

1   'I work very hard and don't enjoy myself much, but when I reach a certain level in the company, or retire, everything will be OK.'

2   'I've enjoyed my career and life so far but now have a feeling that in some ways I wish I had made different choices because where I have ended up could have been better.'

3   'I'm very efficient and I am doing a lot of things at the moment, but I don't seem to be any further forwards in life generally.'

4   'I enjoy life, living from day to day, choosing between options and making decisions when they come up, but unless I have a lucky break I am not likely to achieve anything special.'

The best process, in holiday terms, would be to choose your destination carefully and then find a method of getting there that is reliable and enjoyable. In terms of life, the process is the same: where do I want to go, how will I get there and how will I enjoy getting there? This last point is important, because most of the process is the journey and very little is the arrival. For example, if you were a mountain climber who loved the views from the summits but hated the climbing, you would be spending most of your time failing to enjoy your life.

You have the choice between whether to be passive or active in determining the future path of your life. You can choose

■   'I wonder where my life will lead?'
■   'What shall I do with my life?'

What path do you want to take? Where do you want to be in five years? Do you have a mental picture of what you want your life to be like in the future? Will it be possible to generate both achievement and quality of life at the same time?

This is in essence what this book is about: combining your goals with an efficient way of living, whilst maintaining quality of life along the way. Deciding where you want to go and then having a good system for getting yourself there are the key issues of time management.

WHY IS TIME MANAGEMENT SO IMPORTANT?

Time management is one of life's fundamental skills and is becoming increasingly important as the world speeds up and we run more and more activities in parallel. Time management is not an ideal name, but is the best name we have, for

the ability to use your time on the things that matter.

The things that matter could be anything in the world, so this is a big subject and an important one! Having control of your *time* is much more than having a Filofax and a tidy desk. It is having control of your *life*. Without good use of time you will not achieve your full potential, your life will be frustrating both to you and to others around you, your stress levels will be higher than they need to be and you won't enjoy your time as much as you could do. On a day-to-day level most of us feel vaguely guilty that we waste time or are disorganized or procrastinate, but have somehow found it too difficult to change our habits. We perhaps have a few dreams that we would like to achieve one day. We know we need to be more organized and more effective in our lives. In some areas we already know what we should be doing, but somehow we don't get around to doing it. How can we make these changes happen?

This book will give you the answers you need, but putting them into practice is up to you! Each chapter contains practical ideas that you can put straight into practice and finishes with an action plan to encourage you to do this. If you act on these this book will change your life.

The book is structured in the following format:

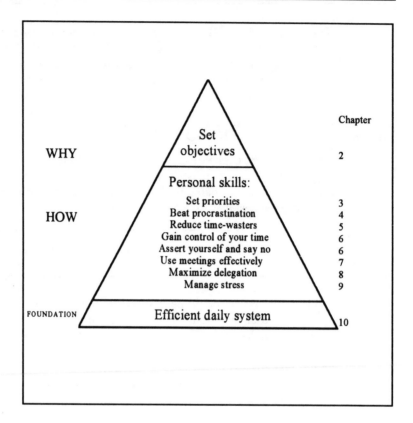

First we will determine your reasons for wanting to use your time better. What will you use your time for? What are your objectives? This is your WHY. Then we will cover a number of skills and techniques that will help you become more productive, use your time more effectively and achieve more of your objectives. These are your HOWs. Finally we will look at your daily routine, the system that you use to control your life. This aspect of time management is the foundation that enables you to use your personal and interpersonal skills, and I have covered it last because until you know where you are going (your strategy) and how you are going to get there (your tactics) there is no point in working out the daily (operational) details.

Without a good personal organization system you won't make any progress, but to focus primarily on daily efficiency would be to miss the point of life. Your daily system is not an end in itself, but simply a tool to take you to where you want to go. That is why the first step must be to consider your objectives.

However, before we define your future objectives in more detail in chapter 2 we need to look at where you are now. This is the subject of chapter 1.

1 Time management: how good is yours?

In this first chapter we will look at your current time management. The chapter is structured as follows:

- definition: achievement and enjoyment
- planning your future
- audit 1: a helicopter view of yourself
- audit 2: how is your day divided up? The work-vs-home dilemma
- audit 3: the outward symptoms of your time management
- too much to do, not enough time?
- audit 4: the key skills
- conclusions.

DEFINITION: ACHIEVEMENT AND ENJOYMENT

Before we can look at performance, we need to be clear what time management is. If we take 'best use of time' as a starting point, your use of time divides into two main areas: achievement and enjoyment. These are linked, in that a sense of achievement will increase your enjoyment of life and, conversely, if you enjoy what you are doing you are more likely to achieve results. This is shown in the diagram below. In situations involving *maximizing* achievement or enjoyment there may also be trade-offs to be made between enjoyment in the present and achievement in the future.

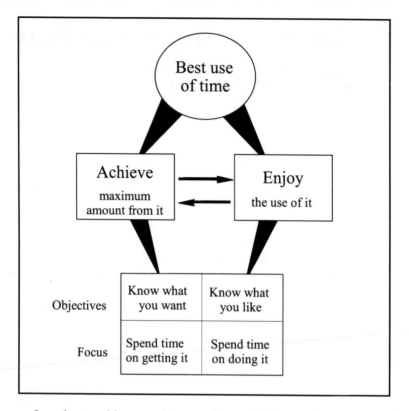

In order to achieve results you will need to know what you want, and then spend time on getting it. Do you know what you want? Are you focused on getting it?

In order to maximize your enjoyment, you need to know what you like and then make sure you spend time on doing it. This may sound obvious, but most people fail to do it. They have feelings about what they like and don't like, but they fail to focus consciously on how they spend their time, letting it be stolen away by time-wasters and unimportant tasks. How much of your time do you spend on the things that you *really* want to do?

The above may sound rather selfish, but you will find that most of your happiness will come from good relationships with others rather than from material things. Therefore, if happiness or peace of mind is one of your goals (either as a process or as a result) you should have 'helping others' or 'making other people happy' as one of your objectives and then make sure you spend time on achieving this.

PLANNING YOUR FUTURE

Achievement requires planning: it's not going to happen by chance.

Returning to the theme of holidays mentioned in the introduction, imagine going on holiday but having no idea of where you are going and no maps. You just drive, taking whichever fork in the road looks more attractive. Would you end up on a secluded sandy beach? Or would you end up in a cul-de-sac only ten miles from where you started? This example sounds far-fetched, yet this is exactly how most of us live our lives. We make career choices and home choices when they crop up, but without any overall major objective or plan of how to get there.

Many companies are also run this way. 'Our product is not selling, let's try something else', 'The competitors have cut their prices, shall we do the same?', 'We're running short of space, shall we extend the building or move?', etc. The central principle of good strategic management is to decide where you want to get to (having assessed where you are and what you're good at) and then plan how to get there.

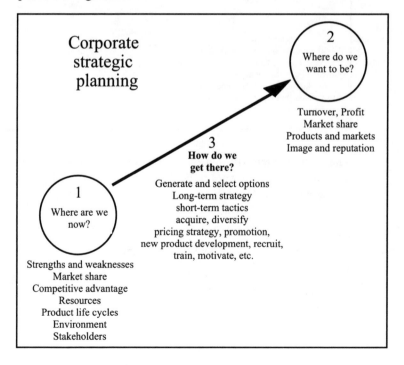

This process can be applied to our own lives, both at work and at home, in exactly the same way.

Personal
strategic
planning

2
Where do I
want to be
in life?

Personal & work
achievements,
relationships,
possessions,
sports and hobbies,
level of stress,
lifestyle, holidays, etc.

3
How do I
get there?

■ Changes in attitudes:
More self-aware
More positive
Think big
Self-discipline
■ Changes in techniques:
Lists
Goal-setting
Organization
Delegation
Assertiveness

1
Where am I
now?

What is good?
What do I enjoy?
What am I good at?
What is not good?
Balance of home vs work
Level of stress
Level of self-organization
Do I know where I'm going?
Am I satisfied with progress to date?
What do I want to change?

The next chapter will help you with stage 2 in the above process, deciding where you want to be. The rest of the book is about stage 3, the process of getting there. But first, let's look at your current situation in global terms.

AUDIT 1: A HELICOPTER VIEW OF YOURSELF

In order to assess your current use of time in global terms, please consider the following questions and put a cross somewhere along the line for each one:

Am I achieving what I want to achieve in life?

Yes,
totally

Not
really

Is everything under control, or am I running in a
hamster wheel and only just keeping up?

Under
control

Only just
keeping up

How much time am I spending on the things that
really matter?

All of
my time

Virtually
none

If I discovered I had only six months to live, how
different would my use of time be?

Change
nothing

Change a
great deal

What is my current stress level, taking home and
work as a total underlying level?

Low

Near
the limit

Do you feel from the above questions that you need to make any
changes?

Next we will look in more detail at how you spend your time.

AUDIT 2: HOW IS YOUR DAY DIVIDED UP? THE WORK-VS-HOME DILEMMA

One of the key indicators for whether you have your life in order is
the balance between work and home, and how happy you are with
it. If you stand back and look at an average day, there is a division
between work and home life. This division could be measured in
actual hours spent, but it could also be described in terms of mental
energy spent on each. For example:

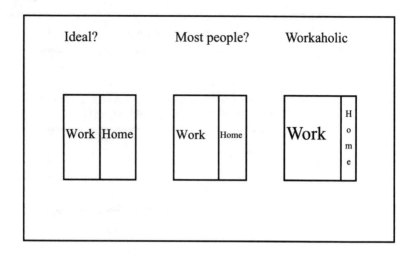

How is *your* day divided up? Draw a line in the diagram below. Is the line where it really ought to be? For many people the demands of work have pushed the line further to the right than it really ought to be. Some would like to be able to spend more time at work, but family pressures prevent this. Deciding where you feel the line really ought to be is important, because if there is an imbalance you can then start to think about how to push it back.

Draw in the vertical line dividing your day between work and home:

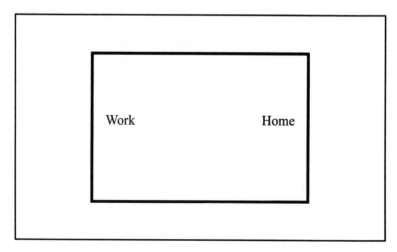

Remember that any time you waste at work will probably end up being time taken away from your family or the outside interests that you would like to be enjoying; the work will still need to be done, so time wasted at work will push the line across into your personal life.

How much productive time at work? How much quality time at home?

Now consider your time spent at work and your time spent at home. Are these frittered away on irrelevant things or are they spent on the things that matter? For many people the balance of time spent looks like this:

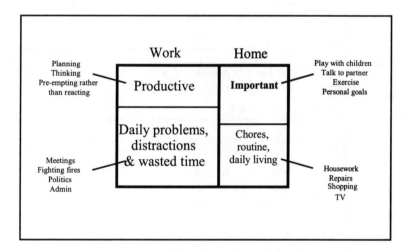

In the above diagram I have given some examples of things that you might feel are irrelevant ('hassle jobs that just have to be done') and things that you might feel are important. But this is a personal decision to be made by you. For example, cooking supper might be an unimportant task that you just have to get done or something important that you enjoy spending time on and learning to become expert at. In chapter 3 we will consider in more detail how to decide whether something really *is* important or not, the ways to handle the urgent 'fire-fighting' jobs that are actually not important in the long term and how to fit in the activities which may not be urgent but are actually important to your quality of life.

What would you put in the boxes in the following diagram; where is your vertical dividing line between work and home, and how high or low would you draw the horizontal dividing lines?

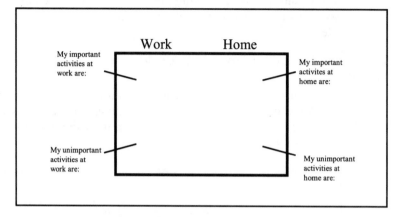

Now you have a picture of your average day. Are you happy with it? Could it be improved?

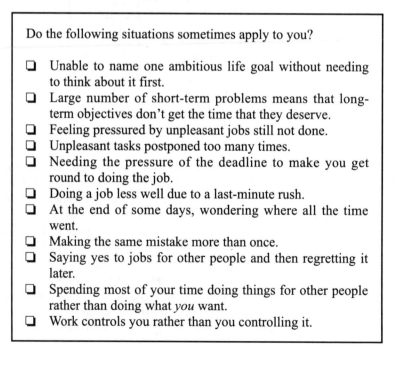

Do the following situations sometimes apply to you?

❑   Unable to name one ambitious life goal without needing to think about it first.

❑   Large number of short-term problems means that long-term objectives don't get the time that they deserve.

❑   Feeling pressured by unpleasant jobs still not done.

❑   Unpleasant tasks postponed too many times.

❑   Needing the pressure of the deadline to make you get round to doing the job.

❑   Doing a job less well due to a last-minute rush.

❑   At the end of some days, wondering where all the time went.

❑   Making the same mistake more than once.

❑   Saying yes to jobs for other people and then regretting it later.

❑   Spending most of your time doing things for other people rather than doing what *you* want.

❑   Work controls you rather than you controlling it.

❏ Thinking about work problems at home.
❏ Not sure what you will achieve tomorrow.
❏ Untidy desk – some jobs have been on it for more than a week.
❏ Forgetting important things/remembering them too late.
❏ Missed deadlines.
❏ Not finishing all the jobs on your 'do' list each day.
❏ Your mental list of jobs that need doing is getting longer and longer.

AUDIT 3: THE OUTWARD SYMPTOMS OF YOUR TIME MANAGEMENT

By the time you finish this book you will have the answers to avoiding all of the above. There are simple techniques you can use which will eradicate all of them from your life. You will probably have noticed the link between time management and stress on the above list; good management of time will have the extra benefit of reducing your stress level, and this is examined in more detail in chapter 9. The last symptom, the list getting longer and longer, is a sign that you are not managing to focus on the things that matter. The next section will look at this in more detail.

TOO MUCH TO DO, NOT ENOUGH TIME?

For most people, the 80/20 rule (or Pareto principle) applies to their time both at home and at work: 80 per cent of their results come from only 20 per cent of their time. This is because only a small part of their total time is spent on their top priorities: for example, at home, quality time with family or friends, and at work, time spent on important proactive activities like thinking and planning. Would it be true in your case to say that at work 80 per cent of your results come from only 20 per cent of your time and that in the rest of your time you do not achieve much?

People with clear tangible products or direct services – for example bricklayers, doctors, teachers or lorry drivers – can perhaps say that all of their time is producing useful results. But even these people may be able to identify wasted time spent waiting for materials, waiting for patients (or dealing with hypochondriacs!), teaching some classes or sitting in traffic. For managers the problem becomes worse, as the productivity of their time is much harder to assess. Results are long term: time spent getting to know and looking after people may or may not be useful, successes and failures may or may not have come about anyway, results depend on the cooperation and abilities of others and are sometimes difficult to measure. Distractions and problems may or may not be important. They are certainly part of your job description, and they may also be a part of the job that you personally regard as rewarding.

If the 80/20 rule applies to you, then you probably feel that you are not spending enough time on the things that are important. Most of your time is either wasted or used on making progress towards your objectives that is too slow. You somehow need to fit everything in, and if the work coming in exceeds the amount being done, then there will be a problem that is getting steadily worse.

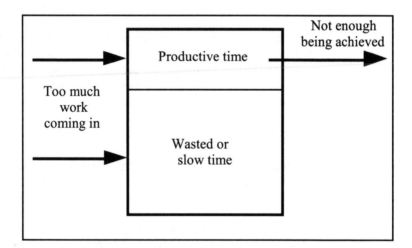

Do you feel that this is you? If so, what can be done? There are in fact ten types of action you can take, as shown in the diagram below. Failure to *choose* one of them will result in one or more of them being forced upon you: probably a longer working day in the short term, failing to achieve your objectives in the longer term, increased stress and also failure to achieve some of the short-term tasks that you need to do.

YOUR TEN OPTIONS

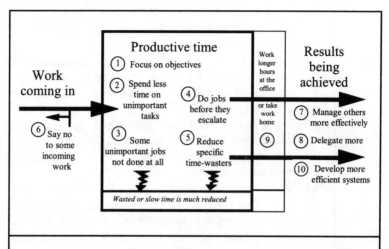

1 Focus clearly on your objectives. This helps you to realize what is important and what is a time-waster, and also helps motivate you to get the necessary work done. Objective-setting is an important activity and is covered in chapter 2.

2 Reduce the time spent on unimportant tasks. Prioritizing and how to handle the daily mix of urgent, non-urgent, important and unimportant tasks is covered in chapter 3. Spending less time on a task that is unimportant could mean doing it less well, and you may need to struggle against your internal driver to 'be perfect' (see chapter 9).

3 Don't do unimportant tasks at all. The difficulty with this option is that the task may be important to someone else, so you may feel morally bound to do it or there may be adverse consequences if you don't do it. If this is the case, take option 2 above. But if the task is self-generated ('I really must trim that hedge') you could consider not doing it. How to decide whether a task really is important or not is covered in chapter 3.

4 If a task is likely to become more serious or more time-consuming with the passing of time, do it sooner rather than later. Methods to help you with overcoming the natur-al tendency to procrastinate are given in chapter 4.

5   Cut down on the time-wasters that are using your potentially productive time. Strategies for doing this are given in chapter 5.

6   Say no to incoming work that is not important to you. An assertive approach to doing this is given in chapter 6.

7   Manage others effectively, both one to one (chapter 6) and in meetings (chapter 7).

8   Delegate more tasks and delegate them more effectively (see chapter 8). This is the only real way to multiply your time and gain major leverage in terms of maximum results from minimum time.

9   Work longer hours. This is not a good strategy, because you will not achieve more by working long hours regularly. If you stay on late and work overtime *once* you will certainly achieve some extra work, but if working overtime or longer hours becomes a habit, then you will end up achieving the same amount but in a longer time. All that has happened is that you have reduced the time you have available for activities outside work: the other half of your life. You could also have increased your stress level (see chapter 9).

10   Develop more efficient systems. Chapter 10 describes the essential components of any personal organization system, without which you will struggle to keep up with the work that is arriving.

Some of these may not be possible for you. None of them is easy. But this is the total number of options that are available to you. If you avoid acting on any of the options you will probably end up taking number 9, the default choice: working longer hours in order to keep up. Since this option *does not work* you will pay the price of higher stress, less achievement and worse quality of life outside work. So in the final audit we need to consider your skills at each of the above.

AUDIT 4: THE KEY SKILLS

Exercise:
Give yourself a mark out of ten for your current competence. This will help you focus on the parts of this book that you really need!

- Awareness of yourself and how well/badly you are using your time   chapter 1

- Knowing clearly what your objectives are   chapter 2

- Ability to spend minimal time on unimportant tasks, even if this means doing them less well   chapter 3

- Being able to cut out the unimportant things that are easy to do or which you feel you *ought* to do   chapter 3

- Doing jobs before they escalate   chapter 4

- Avoiding time-wasters   chapter 5

- Saying no to extra work that is unimportant   chapter 6

- Managing others effectively one to one   chapter 7

- Effective use of meetings   chapter 7

- Delegating   chapter 8

- NOT working long hours regularly   chapter 9

- Efficiency of your personal organization system
                                                chapter 10

CONCLUSIONS

In this chapter we have started with an overview of your life and then zoomed in on how you divide your day and the symptoms you experience during the day. We have defined the key activities and skills that you need in order to be able to make the best use of your time. You can summarize your notes below:

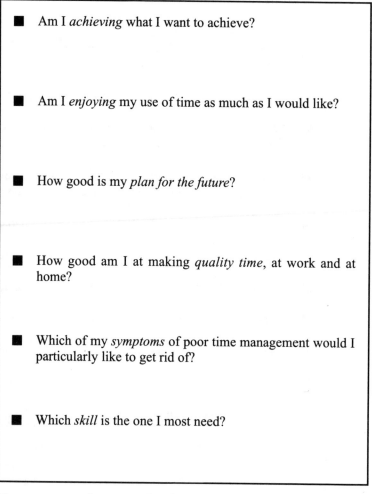

■ Am I *achieving* what I want to achieve?

■ Am I *enjoying* my use of time as much as I would like?

■ How good is my *plan for the future*?

■ How good am I at making *quality time*, at work and at home?

■ Which of my *symptoms* of poor time management would I particularly like to get rid of?

■ Which *skill* is the one I most need?

Now we are ready to start the change process by mapping out your future.

2 Objectives: where do you want to be?

This chapter is about deciding your objectives in life. Some people call these targets or goals, others may call them aspirations or even dreams, but one thing is certain, if you don't know where you're going you will end up *somewhere*, and the chances are that you won't like it when you get there.

This chapter will cover the following areas:

- the power of goal-setting
- defining your objectives
- quality of life: where does it come from?
- fourteen questions you can ask yourself to help clarify your thoughts
- writing objectives down
- the subconscious, and how to use it to your advantage
- pictures and self-talk
- levels of goal-setting power
- enjoying the price
- cutting out negative talk.

THE POWER OF GOAL-SETTING

Ten years ago I read in a magazine that to achieve your dreams you should write them all down, in detail, and read the list every morning when you wake up and every night when you go to sleep. As a logical and scientifically trained Chartered Engineer I could see no way that doing this would make any difference to my future, but the article made me realize that I had no idea where I wanted to be in life, so out of curiosity I compiled a list of the features of my ideal lifestyle. I listed some material things, like exact earnings, exact type and colour of car, etc., but I also wrote down quality-of-life areas. Many of the things I wrote were unlikely dreams that I knew were not reasonable to expect, although they were all theoretically possible and just about imaginable. I also tried reading the list twice a day but soon became bored (I think I lasted about two days), and then I even lost track of where the list was. When I was moving house three years later I found the list, and was totally amazed when I realized that EVERYTHING on the list had happened to me. I asked myself how this could have happened, and I have three possible explanations, which were probably all working in unison:

- better choices: perhaps our subconscious mind works, unknown to us, on the list, making small decisions and choices every day that move us towards our objectives
- improved performance: perhaps the act of visualizing oneself in a successful situation removes blocks to performance and improves ones abilities
- influence over people and events: maybe there is some form of unknown, perhaps spiritual, force at work.

Whilst the first two explanations seem logical and likely, I am extremely reluctant to include the third one, but I must say that many objectives that I have written down since that first list have happened to me, and most of these have involved coincidences and external agencies which I could not have controlled and which have seemed to go beyond mere good luck. There appears to be some scientific evidence that people's minds do affect each other and can also affect physical equipment like electronic random-number generators, even at substantial distances. There are also many serious thinkers (for example Carl Jung) who believe that all of our minds are in some way connected to a Superconscious Mind, so that all knowledge could theoretically be available to us when we are receptive. Meditation, creativity, dreams, and maybe even premonitions, are said to be about tapping into this Superconscious Mind. The Superconscious Mind may be simply the sum of everyone's minds, like a cerebral Internet, or it may be a separate entity in itself, much more powerful than any of us, to which we are all tenuously connected through our own individual subconscious minds. I would recommend M. Scott Peck and Brian Tracy as two interesting authors on this subject.

But in a sense we don't need to know how it works, as long as it *does* work. Try it for yourself! By the end of this chapter you will have written your goals down in detail, just as I did, so your journey will have started.

You decide what is important

The only judge, in the end, of how you should ideally spend your time is yourself. It is vital to think about this and decide on it, rather than running in a hamster wheel without ever questioning it. You may decide you *like* being in the wheel, at least for some of each day or for two days a week. You may decide that really you'd rather be in a different wheel. But once you know where you want to be, you can then set about finding a way to get there. You can focus your energies and your use of time on getting there. You will achieve success, because you will be doing what you want to do, what you enjoy and are good at, and what you feel is important and worthwhile.

But what do we mean by success? There are many definitions, most *not* involving money. Here are two:

- to have achieved the freedom to be able to spend your time in ways that you control
- to have achieved an objective that you personally feel is worthwhile.

What is *your* definition of success? Your first reaction is probably money and fame, but would you really want this for yourself? What is your mental image of yourself as successful, if you have one? For example, let's suppose that fishing is something you really like to do but only have time for occasionally. What would be your image of personal success? Perhaps it is being able, thanks to your business or investments, to go fishing whenever you want, wherever you want, for as long as you want. Perhaps it is being respected as one of the best anglers in the country. Perhaps it is to have caught the largest bream ever, or just one over a certain size. Perhaps it is to have taught thirty children to fish, and to have filled them with enthusiasm to the point where they win competitions. As you can see, your definition of success could well be linked to activities that you enjoy, and could involve helping others, achieving public recognition or simply the freedom to use your time as you wish. So, what is *your* image of success? If you don't have one, you certainly won't achieve it! Take a moment to think about this, now.

DEFINING YOUR OBJECTIVES

It is vital to convert a vague feeling of success into a clear and detailed picture. This will probably involve three areas:

■ work: objectives given to you by your boss
■ work: your own personal agenda at work
■ home: yourself and your family.

Have you clearly defined with your boss what you are employed to achieve? Have you thought about what you *personally* want to achieve at work? Can you achieve the things on this personal agenda and still do what the organization wants? For most of us who are reasonably happy in our jobs there will be a high degree of overlap between our *official* work objectives and our *personal* work objectives.

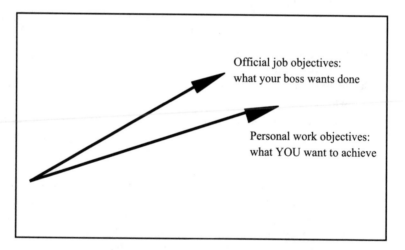

Official job objectives:
what your boss wants done

Personal work objectives:
what YOU want to achieve

Which ones should take priority? I believe that you should concentrate on your *personal* agenda first, because only if you are doing what you enjoy and what you really believe in will you achieve excellent results, and the job objectives will then happen anyway as a result of your enhanced performance. If you work only on your official objectives you will not be as motivated so you will not perform as effectively, and you will also be dissatisfied at not achieving all of your personal goals.

If what you want to achieve at work is significantly different from what your boss wants, then you have a problem: you will either be personally dissatisfied or get fired, so perhaps it is time to think about doing a different job. But before you do, you could consider the question: can your job objectives be renegotiated so that they are nearer to your personal ones?

Other people diverting your progress

Other people have their own priorities and objectives, which often involve *you* spending time helping them achieve these. How much of your time can you afford to spend on other people's priorities and objectives if they do not coincide with your own? At first sight it may appear optimal for you to spend all of your time on your own objectives and say no to everyone else's, but fortunately this is not the case. Clearly give and take is a necessary feature of civilized life, and I believe that there are three reasons why helping others does happen. One is that if you help someone else now, they will be more likely to help you in the future. The second is that partnerships and teams can achieve much more than isolated individuals. The third reason for helping others is that doing so can be enjoyable and is potentially one of the largest sources of pleasure.

So although it is important to know what you want to do, and to make sure you spend the maximum time on achieving it, there is no reason to exclude the ability to help others too. In fact, it is more likely to be true that you can't get what *you* want without helping other people to get what *they* want.

Here are some goal-setting pointers you could use for your work.

GOALS AT WORK

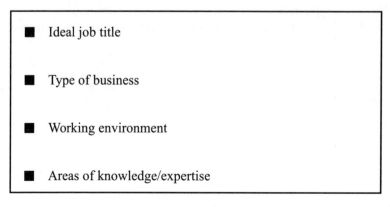

- Ideal job title

- Type of business

- Working environment

- Areas of knowledge/expertise

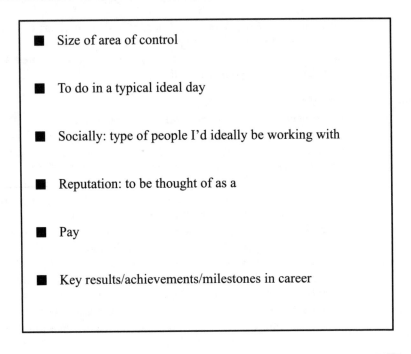

■   Size of area of control

■   To do in a typical ideal day

■   Socially: type of people I'd ideally be working with

■   Reputation: to be thought of as a

■   Pay

■   Key results/achievements/milestones in career

QUALITY OF LIFE

Next, have you considered what it is that gives you your real 'quality of life'? What are the moments when you are able to think to yourself 'Yes, this is what life's all about'? These could be either at work or at home, or some of each.

Exercise:
Write down when you last thought or said 'This is the life!'

These are usually either 'mastery' moments (like hanging back on your windsurfer at high speed with everything just right, or reaching the top of the mountain and seeing the panoramic view on the other side, or reeling in the huge fish after a day of waiting) or 'intimacy' moments (like sitting with a loved one and watching the sun set, with a glass of wine, or watching the children play on the beach).

Quality of life may come from physical pleasures or mental ones (including spiritual), as shown by the examples in the circles in the following diagram:

QUALITY OF LIFE

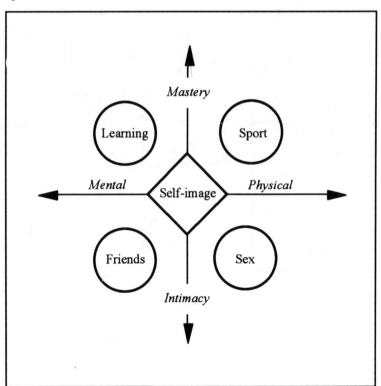

Your self-image is also important to your quality of life: it is affected by both your physical and mental images of yourself, which in turn are affected by your achievements (mastery) and the success or otherwise of the relationships you have (intimacy). The resulting self-image then governs your ability to achieve further mastery and intimacy, both physically and mentally. Later in this chapter we will look more closely at the role of self-talk and the subconscious in improving your self-image and thus your ability to improve the quality of your life. The results of a good self-image and getting the balance right between the physical and mental aspects, and the mastery and intimacy aspects, will be a combination of achievement, fun, happiness and peace of mind.

QUALITY OF LIFE

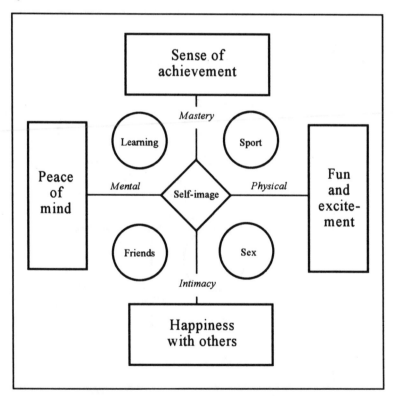

If the balance is not right you could be spending too much time on achieving results, perhaps at work, at the expense of personal relationships and peace of mind. This situation is examined in more detail in chapter 9, when we look at stress. Conversely, you may have a contented and secure lifestyle but be lacking a feeling of excitement and/or achievement. Another imbalance would be to neglect the physical or the mental sides of life, or perhaps even to have such poor time management that you neglect *all* of the key areas because you find yourself using all of your time just getting by. In chapter 3 we will see how the unimportant tasks can take time away from the important ones, and certainly time spent on these quality-of-life areas is very important.

So, when considering your goals outside work you may wish to consider the above categories and the balance between them. In which areas could you improve the quality of your life at present?

Here are some goal-setting pointers you could consider for your personal life.

GOALS OUTSIDE WORK

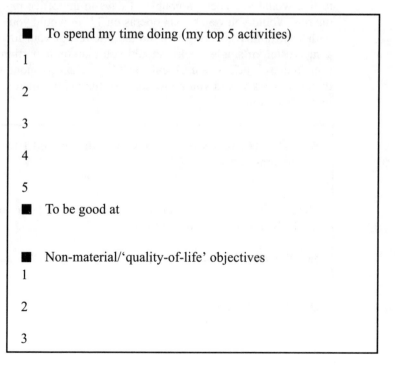

■ To spend my time doing (my top 5 activities)

1

2

3

4

5

■ To be good at

■ Non-material/'quality-of-life' objectives

1

2

3

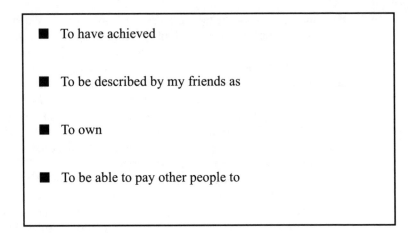

■ To have achieved

■ To be described by my friends as

■ To own

■ To be able to pay other people to

THE ULTIMATE QUESTION

An interesting way to consider the relative importance of work and family is to consider the following situation: if you had only a week to live would you spend a couple of days in the office replying to memos, would you watch soap operas on TV or would you spend it with your family? Bearing in mind that the rest of your life is only a succession of single weeks, should you plan on apportioning the time in these weeks in a different way? If you had six months rather than one week would you allow some of the unimportant activities to creep back in?

■ What changes would I make if I discovered I had six months to live?

Here are some other major questions that may help you to think about what's important to you.

■ What are the five things I value most in my life?

■ What am I good at?

■ What would I do if I won a £1 million tomorrow?

■ Whose personality or lifestyle would I like to copy, and why?

■ If I could write a 'film script' for the next five years of my life what would I write for myself?

■ What have I always wanted to do but always been afraid to try?

■ What one thing would I do if I knew I could not fail?

■ What have I always wanted to do but not had time to do?

■ What makes me wake up thinking 'Great, it's . . . x . . . today'?

■ During the last week, what has made me feel good?

■ What do I wish to avoid (then rephrase it as a positive goal)?

■ What would I like to spend my time doing when I retire (and can I start doing some of these things now)?

■ What epitaph would I want written on my gravestone?

As a result of thinking about the above questions, you should now have a list of between five and twenty goals. They will be a mixture of material things, relationships, quality-of-life ideas and thoughts on how you would ideally spend your time. Some will be short term, some will be long term. You should have a mental picture of what your ideal life would be like. Now let's refine this list a little. The objectives that you choose for yourself should be

- BIG: big enough to feel like a step change rather than a small continuation of progress, big enough to be worth making an effort to reach, big enough to stretch you.
- EXCITING: if your goals don't excite you they won't happen. Do they conjure up a vivid mental picture? Are they worth some effort?
- SERIOUS: you have to *really want* them. For example, I'd quite like a Ferrari (I wouldn't say no to one anyway!) but I'm not *passionate* about one. I don't go and press my nose to the glass of the showroom window on a Sunday afternoon. I don't know all the different model numbers and how many of each were made. So it would be no good my writing down 'to have a Ferrari' as one of my goals: my subconscious knows it's not a serious goal to me, so it wouldn't happen.
- CLEAR: your subconscious needs to know exactly what your goal is, since it cannot cope with abstract or fuzzy ideas.

Instead of 'to have a better job', your goal should be to get a particular job with a particular company. What will your office be like? How much will you be paid? What will a typical working day be like? In order to get these details clear you may need to do some research, which will then be the first step towards achieving the goal. Instead of planning 'to get a BMW one day', you should know the model, engine size and colour clearly enough to be able to visualize an exact picture. This could involve visiting a dealer or even going for a test drive! Instead of 'getting fit', your fitness goal should be to be able to run a known distance or perform an exact number of exercises in a certain time. Your subconscious now has a target to work on, and an 'internal success video' that it can view and make real.

YOUR SUBCONSCIOUS

I would like to make a brief digression here into an examination of the power of the subconscious, which has to be understood before you can focus on your objectives properly. The subconscious part of your mind, not the conscious part, is what controls your behaviour. How you feel in situations, how you react, the decisions you make, and the physical and mental capabilities that you have are all being run by this inner part of your brain. It is impossible to behave consistently in a way that is different from the way you see yourself. You can put on an act and temporarily fool others, but your real self soon shows. This 'real self' is controlled by your subconscious mind. Your attitudes and beliefs, whether they are positive or negative, will have much more effect on your future success than your intelligence or your natural talents. By influencing your subconscious, which controls your attitudes and beliefs, you can make the results happen.

■ *Example*: why was John MacEnroe the best tennis player in the world in 1983? He probably wasn't the strongest, fastest or cleverest person in the tournaments, but something inside him knew how to swing the racquet just right. He had something different in his subconscious.

■ *Example*: the four-minute mile was believed to be physically impossible for years, until Roger Bannister finally achieved it. The next year thirty-seven people broke the four-minute barrier, and the year after that 300! People did not change physically in only two years, but their mental pictures did.

■ *Example*: some people cannot speak in public without sweating and forgetting their words, while others find it easy. There is no difference in intelligence or ability – it's whether your subconscious is saying 'I can't' or 'I can'.

■ *Final example*: memory – do you find that as soon as someone is introduced to you you forget their name? Have you ever sat in an examination and been unable to remember the answer to a question, even though you went to the lecture and understood it at the time? Whether or not you can retrieve the information, which is certainly in your brain because you'll recognize it if you see or hear it again, is down to whether your *subconscious* lets it out.

You may have noticed that sometimes your subconscious is working when you are doing something else or going to sleep: suddenly the answer to a problem or a name you have been trying to remember pops into your mind. You can't force your subconscious to work, you just have to let it.

Can we manipulate our subconscious to make ourselves better at remembering names, speaking in public or even playing tennis? Yes! In 1984 Alan Richardson carried out an experiment involving two groups of basketball players, one practising all week and the other sitting in comfortable chairs thinking about the ball falling perfectly into the hoop. In trials at the end of the week the second group, the thinkers, had improved more! Similarly, when you play tennis you should visualize the perfect shot before you hit the ball and again after any mistakes. The golfer Jack Nicklaus is one of many professionals who use pre-visualization to achieve better putts.

The two best ways to reprogramme your subconscious for success are pictures and words.

Pictures

Paint mental pictures of the desired situation. This works both for the short term and the long term. You can experience a simple example of the short-term principle of 'what you see is what you get' by putting a plank on the ground and walking along it. You visualize yourself walking along it easily, and that is exactly what you do. Now put the plank between two high buildings, and suddenly it is not so easy to walk along! This is because you are now visualizing yourself falling off it, and that is probably what will happen. The plank is the same, your balance skills are the same, but your subconscious has a very different picture and is controlling your behaviour differently.

Here are two practical examples of visualization at work.

■ When you are preparing to give an important talk to a large audience don't imagine the talk going terribly wrong, with you drying up and having to leave the stage hurriedly. Instead, picture the crowd applauding your brilliant public speech and queueing up to shake your hand afterwards. You will give a much better talk.

■ When visiting an important customer to ask for business don't imagine them saying 'No thanks, we're not interested', but instead picture them saying 'That's great, I'll order ten! When can I have them?'

Do these pictures simply make *you* perform better, or do they in some way influence the other person too? No one knows, but as long as they work perhaps we don't need to know.

For longer-term goals, either material, quality-of-life or self-improvement, cut out pictures and put them somewhere that you will see them every day, like on your fridge or bathroom mirror. These could be pictures of houses, empty beaches representing freedom, an organized desk, yourself spending time with your family, or anyone you admire – sportsmen/women, businessmen/women, people of character, whatever – or perhaps if slimming or exercise is your goal, your head cut out and glued on to a perfectly slim/muscular body. These pictures will constantly remind your subconscious of your objectives and will supply it with every detail of the required result in a much more powerful way than mere words. Your subconscious mind works in pictures and will readily absorb these images.

Words

Ninety-nine per cent of the talking you do is talking to yourself, so make it good! Say to yourself 'I have a great memory for names', 'Public speaking is easy and fun for me', or 'The golf ball always goes exactly where I want it to go'. At first these words will sound silly, because your subconscious is disagreeing with the words that your conscious is saying and the images that your conscious is forcing your brain to project, and is trying to reject them (technically this internal conflict is known as cognitive dissonance). As a powerful example of this feeling, try saying out loud to yourself 'I'm the best!' Did you feel odd in your stomach? That was cognitive dissonance, because your subconscious mind did not accept the statement as true.

Your subconscious can only tell truth from lies by comparing new information with the memory bank of all your life's experiences, so if you have never been the best, or have never thought of yourself a such, it now has this idea fixed. But like a huge supertanker your subconscious can be slowly steered around, by repeated nudges. If you say 'I'm the best' every day, your subconscious will start to believe it. You can build your self-image in this simple way and be more successful at anything you do. (This should not be confused with arrogance, which is a manifestation of *poor* self-image, not healthy self-image, so saying 'I'm the best' will not make you think any less of others.)

A VIEW OF HOW YOUR BRAIN WORKS

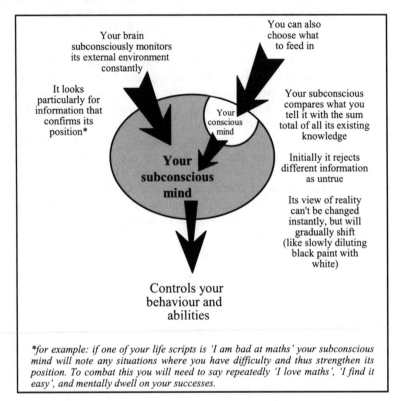

You brain
subconsciously monitors
its external environment
constantly

You can also
choose what
to feed in

It looks
particularly for
information that
confirms its
position*

Your
conscious
mind

Your subconscious
compares what you
tell it with the sum
total of all its existing
knowledge

Initially it rejects
different information
as untrue

**Your
subconscious
mind**

Its view of reality
can't be changed
instantly, but will
gradually shift
(like slowly diluting
black paint with
white)

Controls your
behaviour and
abilities

*for example: if one of your life scripts is 'I am bad at maths' your subconscious mind will note any situations where you have difficulty and thus strengthen its position. To combat this you will need to say repeatedly 'I love maths', 'I find it easy', and mentally dwell on your successes.

You can design your own self-talk phrases, but some good ones I recommend to everyone are:

■ first thing in the morning: 'I feel *great* today'
■ then as you look in the bathroom mirror: 'I *like* myself'
■ and as you travel to work: 'I *love* my work.'

They may seem ridiculous at first, but try them! They will become true in a matter of days.

Some more personal self-talk phrases might be

■ I find computers easy to use
■ I enjoy meeting new people
■ my house is always clean and neat
■ my desk is always tidy

- I am always on time
- I don't get angry when people keep me waiting
- I like my boss and he likes me
- I find it easy to say no when I need to.

If your subconscious mind has been holding you back (perhaps because it has been programmed by other people saying 'You'll never do that'), repeating these phrases to yourself will remove the ceiling on your performance. You will then be able to behave in a way that is consistent with achieving your goals, and the real results of your performance will 'catch up' with your internal image of those results already having been achieved.

Finally on the subject of the subconscious, I would like to add that your subconscious can only see positive concepts. If you say to yourself 'I am going to watch less TV' or 'I am going to smoke less', your subconscious only sees TV and smoking! This is why most New Year's resolutions fail. You need to give your subconscious a clear picture. For example, 'I read for an hour every evening, go for a walk and then go to bed early' or 'I can't stand cigarettes, they make me feel sick'. These conjure up pictures in your mind, and although the smoking example may not sound very 'positive', it does produce an image that can be clearly visualized. If you repeat these statements regularly, at least twice a day and if necessary up to a hundred times, your subconscious will come to accept them and they will rapidly become true descriptions of your behaviour.

Is this brainwashing? Yes, I suppose it is, but at least you are in control of where you are going, and you can choose to make the destination a good one for both yourself and others. Positive self-brainwashing is certainly better than the usual negative brainwashing that we all tend to use on ourselves and on others. Nobody has a problem with other people saying 'I can never get this right' or 'Typical, I always forget that' or 'You won't find that easy', so why is it regarded as strange to say positive things like 'I always succeed at this', or 'I can do this if I want to' or 'You can do it, I know you can'? You can decide, today, whether you want to talk yourself and others *up* or talk yourself and others *down*.

So, to sum up progress so far in this chapter, you have thought about your objectives, both small and large, short term and long term, and you have seen how your subconscious controls your behaviour and abilities and therefore controls your ability to achieve your objectives. You have seen how your subconscious works on a combination of the pictures it sees and the words it hears. In order to use your subconscious in the best way to achieve your objectives it is necessary to write your objectives down, refresh them every day in order to keep your subconscious on track, set dates for the goals to ensure progress at a rapid rate, have a plan of the steps along the way and then enjoy the price of achieving the plan. Each of these will be considered in more detail next.

WRITE YOUR GOALS DOWN

If you don't write your objectives down, you have not told your subconscious that you are really committed to them. Don't worry, you don't have to show your list to anyone else! In fact, I would recommend keeping your list of goals to yourself, or at least only showing them to others who have done the same. Negative and apathetic people will drag you down very fast. If someone says 'You'll never achieve that' your subconscious believes it and makes it true.

Refresh them every day

This is the repetition part mentioned above, to steer the supertanker of your subconscious by a series of small nudges. It involves seeing pictures on your wall and reading your list of goals every day, picturing in your mind what achieving them will be like and saying out loud 'I am . . .' or 'I have achieved . . .' This takes time and may be boring to your *conscious* mind, but is well worth the two minutes a day that it takes.

At the start of this chapter I described how I made a list of goals and realized three years later (to my amazement) that they had all happened to me. I use the phrase 'happened to me' because many of them were not achieved as a result of direct effort on my part. I didn't carry out the recommended daily refreshing activity of reading the list first thing every morning and last thing every night, feeling that this would be too superstitious and probably too boring as well. I also didn't set dates or have a plan of how to get there. Yet I still achieved all of my list! I now believe that this is like setting your course and then not looking at the map and not monitoring your speed: you *may* get there, but there is a high risk that you will drift off course.

The diagram below shows that there are different levels of seriousness that you can choose for your goal-setting; I recommend the top one as the most powerful, but it does take some discipline to follow and the choice is up to you.

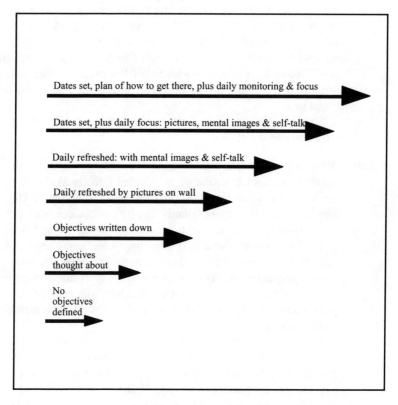

As you can see, the top two arrows involve setting dates for your goals, and the very top one involves having a plan as well.

Set dates for your goals

A goal without a date is just an idle wish: 'Some day I'd like to go to Australia' is very different from 'I'm going to Australia next year', and 'I'll be a director by the age of thirty' is very different from 'One day I'll be a director'. Setting a date forces your subconscious to start working on it. It is unable to procrastinate and get away with 'I'll start on that next year'. It knows you are serious.

Since your subconscious is perhaps the *real you*, by setting a date on your goals you are telling yourself that you really are serious about achieving them.

Why do so few people write their goals down and set dates for them? Why is it a rather uncomfortable feeling to set a date? The answer is FEAR OF FAILURE. Once you have admitted to yourself that you want to achieve those things, you run the risk of failing and having to admit to yourself that you are a failure. But are you? Suppose you only achieve half the progress that you aimed for, you are still ahead of where you would have been without setting a goal.

So take courage, write your goals down, set dates and get serious. You can do it!

Have a plan of how to get there

Your objectives can probably be divided into chunks or steps along the way. What are the sub-tasks you need to achieve? Objectives like 'get fit', 'have more friends' or 'be more successful at my job' are too large easily to visualize getting started on and need to be divided into steps. The initial steps might be 'join a tennis club', or 'talk to a new person every day' or 'read one book per week on my chosen success area'. This is, in a way, project managing your life, and although it may seem rather mechanistic, remember that the tasks should be fun in their own right as well as contributing to your overall plan.

Some of the steps along the way will appear to be hard work, or at least to require some effort. Is your objective worth it? In his classic book *See You at the Top*, Zig Ziglar says: 'Either you can pay the price of success, or you WILL pay the price of failure.' What he means is that apathy now will cost you regret later, and taking the easy road now will mean more difficulty later. You will need to do some work, to pay some sort of price. Are you prepared to pay it? Fortunately, taking the apparently harder road will be more satisfying along the way, in addition to producing a better outcome!

Enjoy the price

It is important to enjoy the price, which is the journey to where you want to be, since this makes up 99 per cent of the process. Only a tiny fraction of life is the moment when you arrive. As soon as you have arrived you will be setting off on another journey to a new destination, so you may as well enjoy the travelling! Management is identical to life in this respect; enjoy the process, because that's what management really is. Both at work and in your home life you only have the present, and your whole life or career is made up of tiny instants, a continuous series of 'nows'; if these are not fun or enjoyable then you will eventually be left with nothing. A measurable result at the end will not be able to make up for a long period of unpleasant effort. This philosophy can be summed up by the saying 'life is a journey, not a destination', which is also sometimes phrased as '*success* is a journey, not a destination'.

Whether you enjoy something depends partly on whether you focus on the good parts of it or the bad parts. For example, we can all think of parties that we didn't enjoy because we 'weren't in the mood'. It wasn't the party that was different, it was something within us. If you try, there are plenty of unpleasant things to focus on at a party!

Enjoyment can also depend on mental scripts. For example, you may have a script like 'I don't like swimming' or 'I don't like opera' programmed into your subconscious. This has been confirmed as true in your subconscious every time you go swimming or hear opera music and don't like it. You may have a dislike of your job, or of part of it, also programmed in. As discussed earlier in this chapter, this programming can be broken by saying to yourself 'I love swimming/opera/my work' regularly and visualizing enjoying it.

If you can enjoy as much of every day as possible, you are 'squeezing more of the juice' out of life, surely a worthwhile objective!

However, sometimes the problem is more than just a matter of opinion (like opera or swimming). The price of success really is tough. Luckily, it is possible to enjoy *any* price if your attitude is right.

Here are some examples of prices you have to pay to get the result you want and views you might take on paying that price.

Area	Desired result	Negative view of price	Positive view of price
Fitness training	Feel fit	Unpleasant, hard work, boring	Invigorating, exhilarating, satisfying, a progression
Negotiating	Obtain best possible settlement	Squalid and frustrating; you always wonder if you could have got more	A fascinating game; you always win something
Recruitment interviewing	Select most suitable employee	Time-consuming, nervous; never really know what they are like, have to reject all except one	Meet new people, a chance to shape the future of the company, a chance to offer someone a job
Giving staff appraisals	Communicate performance to staff and agree targets	Embarrassing, dishonest, unpleasant if bad news has to be given	Important, worthwhile, a chance to shape someone's future for the best
Presentation to a group of important people	Communicate message	Frightening, risky; what if it goes wrong? What if they ask a question I can't answer?	A chance to impress, get what you want, feel good after it went well, be the expert on your particular subject
Cold call to potential customer	Achieve a sale or the first step towards a sale	They might be rude; I'll get depressed; is this job worth doing?	Learning about people, developing my skills, achieving sales target; what will I do with the bonus?

Clearly, if you develop the habit of enjoying the price there ceases to be a noticeable price to pay. You are therefore much more likely to continue to make the effort required to achieve your objectives.

One idea that is particularly useful in developing this success habit is: NEVER SAY ANYTHING NEGATIVE. This is not easy! Think about most conversations – the weather, traffic jams, the latest murder or war that was on the news, changes in the company – they are usually negative.

■ bad things in the past are best forgotten, so don't drag a burden of grudges and regret around with you

■ bad things in the present are best ignored – it's better to smell the roses than to look at the manure

■ bad things in the future can be spoken into existence, so don't dwell on potential problems – have a contingency plan, yes, but think positive.

Exercise:
Here are some classic negative phrases and habits that you could try to banish from your life. As you read each one, think of a positive alternative that you could use instead?

Negative phrase   *Positive alternative*

'I bet it doesn't work'

'If only I'd . . .'

'He'll probably be late'

'You'll never manage that'

'I hope it doesn't break down'

'Typical'

'The world isn't fair/there's no justice'

'Sod's law'

'I can't believe I was so stupid'

Criticizing others behind their backs

Bearing grudges

To a child:

'Your room is always such a
mess'

'Don't run out in front of a car'

'Be careful not to lose it'

■   Here are some positive phrases that you could try instead.

Negative phrase	Positive alternative
'I bet it doesn't work'	'This time it will work'
'If only I'd . . .'	'Next time I will . . .'
'He'll probably be late'	'I'll make sure he's on time by . . .'
'You'll never manage that'	'You can do it!'
'I hope it doesn't break down'	'I've got some spares but I won't need them'
'Typical'	'How can I prevent a repeat of this?'

'The world isn't fair/there's no justice'	'I am responsible for what happens to me'
'Sod's law'	'It's lucky it didn't happen at a more critical moment'
'I can't believe I was so stupid'	'Next time I will check for . . .'
Criticizing others behind their backs	Praise others behind their backs
Bearing grudges	Forgive them (it's just how they are) and plan how to prevent a repeat

To a child:

'Your room is always such a mess'	'I like it when you tidy your room'
'Don't run out in front of a car'	'Stay on the pavement'
'Be careful not to lose it'	'Always put it back in the box straight afterwards'

How can you get into the habit of avoiding the negative phrases and using positive ones instead? You could try making a contract with someone close to you, perhaps your wife/husband or a work colleague, to point out whenever you say something negative. For a while I played a game with my wife where I had to contribute 50p to her collection if she caught me saying anything negative (and vice versa), our collections to be spent on whatever luxury we wanted. This simple game made me much more positive, thus allowing me to enjoy life more and achieve more, and I gained much more than I paid!

ACTION POINTS

Tick the ones you feel you ought to do.

- ❏ List your goals at work.
- ❏ Compare with your job specification and renegotiate if necessary.
- ❏ List your goals for your personal life.
- ❏ Visualize your ideal life.
- ❏ Get pictures.
- ❏ Design and use about ten self-talk phrases.
- ❏ Refresh goals daily: mentally picture and speak.
- ❏ Set dates on goals.
- ❏ Divide into sub-tasks.
- ❏ Resolve to enjoy the price.
- ❏ Begin a no-negatives campaign.

3 Prioritizing: is it urgent? Is it important?

In this chapter we will be looking at the first step towards organizing your day. We will look at how to achieve a balance between the short-term urgent jobs and the long-term important ones, so that you can both cope and move forward.

The structure of the chapter is:

■ what do urgent and important really mean?
■ what are the effects of the four combinations of importance and urgency?
■ how do I plan all the types of task into my day?

Let's assume that you have a list of jobs that you intend to do and that many other tasks and problems will crop up during the day. What is the best way to categorize these tasks to allow you to organize this work?

URGENCY

How *urgent* a job is should define *when* you do it. Prioritizing your jobs into order is based on the times at which each needs to be completed. This should be your first action: number each job to show the order in which you will do them. This sounds simple, but have you done it? Have you got a list of the jobs you need to do today or tomorrow, numbered in order? Often, urgency is defined by *other people's* need for completion of that job, and is therefore not related to your own personal view of its importance.

IMPORTANCE

Always remember that this is independent of urgency! The importance of a job defines *how long* you should spend on it. Quite separately from the urgency of each job, you can assign an importance to it: high, medium or low, or a number up to ten. Try this for your list of current jobs to be done. You can see that it is very quick and easy – it takes one minute at the most.

Often, importance is defined by your internal judgement, not by other people. How do you decide if a job is important?

Exercise:

■   List three jobs you need to do today.

1

2

3

■   Write against each one how important it is, out of 10.

■   Now think about what basis you used to make this judgement.

You will probably find that you 'just know' which one is the most important. But how? The answer is that the important jobs are the ones that *move you towards your goals*, which you defined in the previous chapter. If it doesn't move you towards one of your goals, then why are you doing it?

Of course, we all have to do things that we don't want to do. Maybe it is part of our job description, or something trivial but unavoidable (like the washing up). Obviously we still have to do these things, but they are not important so they should be given as little time as possible. If a way could be found to avoid doing them at all, it should be found. Remember that everything new we do means *not* doing something else, and the unimportant jobs should be the ones to go.

A method that I sometimes use for deciding whether a job is *really* important or not is as follows: think to yourself, 'If I had a red button on my desk which I could press and which would instantly make the job complete, would I press the button?' Try it for the following examples, asking yourself if you would like these jobs to be done, magically and instantly, by someone else:

- the washing up
- catching a fish in the local river
- travelling by motorcycle to a destination five miles away
- playing football and scoring three goals
- mowing the lawn
- writing a sales report on performance for the year to date
- coaching a subordinate and being thanked for helping them
- sitting in the sun with your partner, looking at the garden
- cooking an unusual recipe
- touring the Greek islands.

As you can see, this method makes it very clear what you enjoy doing and what you feel is worthwhile use of your time. Did you choose to press the red button to avoid the motorcycle journey and instantly arrive, or did you choose to spend some time travelling on the open road? There isn't a right answer: it's a matter of opinion, depending on what you personally enjoy and want to spend time doing. If the *result* is what you want, but you don't want to spend the *time* on getting it, then it does not qualify as important! It may be urgent, and it may be important to someone else, and you may not be able to avoid doing it, but it's still not important to YOU.

In the fishing example in the above list, you may want the fish to eat and not want to bother with sitting on the river bank for hours to get it; this means that although eating may be important to you, fishing is not. Your objective is then to minimize the time taken to get the fish. For others, the process of fishing is what is important, and eating a fish they took some time to catch is all the better.

As discussed in chapter 2, when there is no alternative but to do the work in order to get the result you need it is worthwhile cultivating the attitude of enjoying the *process*.

- as well as enjoying eating the fish, you could learn to enjoy sitting and waiting for it to bite
- as well as enjoying the compliments on the decorated room, it is possible to enjoy the process of painting and wallpapering too.

After all, 99 per cent of any activity is the journey and only 1 per cent is arriving!

FOUR TYPES OF TASK

If everything was either 'urgent and important' (the top job, which you must do right now) or 'non-urgent and unimportant' (jobs which don't matter and you can do later) life would be simple. But in fact most jobs fall into the other two categories, shown as boxes 2 and 3 below.

	Important	*Not important*
Urgent	1 Urgent and important Real crises Some avoidable if you had prepared or planned Some unforeseeable Also: major opportunities for pleasure or progress Do it now!	2 Urgent but unimportant Reactive jobs Rush jobs Unexpected problems Other people's work Done to avoid trouble Spend minimum time on it or delegate it
Not urgent	3 Not urgent but important Can wait until tomorrow or next week, but will certainly need to be done some time Failing to do these will mean missed opportunities Plan it	4 Neither urgent nor important Tempting and easy jobs Irrelevant jobs Unpleasant long-term tasks Don't do it (unless it's likely to escalate, in which case plan it, and plan to spend the minimum time on it)

> Urgency: *when* the task has to be done.
> Importance: *how much* time should be allocated to the task.

This diagram shows Yes or No rather than a continuum, and this is obviously simplified; for example, urgent could mean do within 30 seconds (angry customer on phone), do within the next hour (visitor arriving later) or do today (boss requires information for a meeting tomorrow). But these four categories are still extremely useful. You'll have to do some box 1 and 2 jobs, and you'll probably want to do some box 4 jobs, and you will need to make the effort to fit in some box 3 jobs if you want the future to work out well. But what mix should we aim for, and which jobs should be done when?

In order to answer this we will now explore each of the four types, taking a closer look at how to handle each one before coming up with an overall system.

CATEGORY 1: IMPORTANT AND URGENT

Clearly these are the top jobs, which need to be done now and done thoroughly. These should be rare, less than one a day! Such jobs might be

- crisis in the factory
- safety hazard discovered
- angry customer demanding answers
- board report due by lunchtime
- problem with shipment just leaving
- teenage son held at police station.

If your life is a constant stream of these then you are not planning ahead enough. You are leaving jobs in box 3 (for doing later) for so long that they become urgent and move into box 1. In fact, you can see from the above list that this is not the sort of life that most people would want to lead, and if they did it would probably not last as long as they would like!

You may also be leaving jobs in box 2 until they become important, although this is less likely because, generally speaking, either a job is important or it is not, either it is going to affect your objectives or it's not. Unless your objectives change, a job cannot move across to the other side. For example, filling up with petrol will become increasingly urgent, but will never become important.

If you have a never-ending succession of jobs in box 1, how will you find the time to get ahead of the game? As mentioned at the end of chapter 1, you could work longer hours, but you are then tackling the symptom and not the cause. If you do this you will find that even your overtime fills up with box 1 tasks. You must tackle the cause itself, which is your inability to plan ahead (box 3) and your inability to distinguish what is important from what is not (boxes 2 and 4). We need to look at this central issue of *importance* next.

CATEGORY 2: URGENT BUT NOT IMPORTANT

The vast majority of jobs which land on your desk each day will be of this type. These are jobs like

- sort out a replacement for someone who is away sick
- get a broken machine fixed
- pay the bills
- reorder stock when levels are low
- disciplinary problems
- most incoming phone calls
- filling up your car with petrol.

You may feel that some of these are important. But are they? Certainly there will be all sorts of consequences if you don't do them, but that doesn't make them important. The definition of important as 'serious consequences if you don't do it' appears logical until you realize that almost every trivial task will have serious consequences if you ignore it. What if you don't wash? What if you don't replace light bulbs when they blow? What if you don't go to the supermarket? I much prefer the *positive* equivalent of the definition: will doing this task raise your life above the level of mere maintenance, towards achieving your objectives? For example, were you born to fill up your car with petrol? Do you wish you could spend more time filling up, perhaps several hours a day? Do you get great enjoyment from the process? Was 'to be an expert tank-filler' on your list of objectives? (If yes, that's your choice, and that's OK, but the answer is probably no!)

If you are really ruthless about focusing on your objectives you will realize that most jobs don't affect them. Ask yourself, 'If I don't do this, will it matter in five years time?' If not, then it's not important. Of course, you *still need to do it*, because if you didn't do any of them you would probably be dead or become unemployed in a lot less than five years, but the point is that these jobs only deserve to have the *minimum* time spent on them. Box 2 is not about deciding *whether* to do the job, but deciding *how much time* to allocate to it. (Delegating these tasks is another option you should consider, and this will be discussed fully in chapter 8.) If you don't spend the minimum time on these tasks, or delegate them, you will not have enough time to do the important jobs which will make your life better in the future.

Some people have no problem with spending the minimum time on jobs, but others are uncomfortable with it.

Why would someone spend longer than strictly necessary on a job?

For one of the following reasons:

- they think it's important (when really it's only urgent)
- they think it's important to *them* because it's important to *someone else*
- they want the job to be done *well*
- they enjoy doing it.

If the time spent in box 2 is to be minimized, we need to feel certain that all four of these are invalid reasons. Let's look at each in turn.

Urgent, mistaken for important

As described above, this is an easy mistake to make, but always keep in the back of your mind that just because you *have* to do the job, this doesn't mean it is deserving of time, effort or quality.

Important to someone else, but not to you

First, realize that it's not important to you, by reference to your objectives. Then decide: 'Do I need to do this job at all, or should I say no to it?' As we have seen, box 2 jobs often do have to be done, even though they are not important. If this is the case, think about whether the job could be delegated. If it really must be done by you (ask yourself 'What if I was on holiday or away for a while, who would do it then?'), think about how it could be done in the *mini-*

mum time to satisfy the other person. Customers and your boss need special treatment, but there will be many other cases where the minimum will suffice.

The job needs to be done properly

Have you ever heard the expression 'If a job's worth doing, it's worth doing well'? What does 'well' mean? As well as you can or well enough? It is important to realize that you cannot do every job perfectly. If you try to, you will probably end up working very long hours and *still* making mistakes. Every job you try to do perfectly means that something else, quite possibly something important, is not done at all.

Am I condoning shoddy work? Not at all! Care, and attention to detail, especially where customers are involved, is vital. Spending the minimum time on something means being *effective*, or doing a Ford rather than a Rolls-Royce job. Although the Rolls-Royce is better made, most people would feel that the Ford is better value for money. The concept of 'value for money' also applies to 'value for time'. There isn't enough time to do every job perfectly, so you can't give everyone perfect service. If every car was a Rolls-Royce many of us would be unable to own a car; similarly, if you try to do every job perfectly there will be many jobs that you don't have time to do at all.

The answer is to have different quality levels for each activity, the levels depending on the degree of importance to you. The most important jobs will involve you constantly striving to get better and better; the less important ones will involve you finding quicker and easier ways to get them done, perhaps even negotiating to relax the standards.

The job is fun

The rule is that it's OK to have fun as long as box 3 is not reduced. Fun jobs are not often found in box 2, since lazy fun tends to be in box 4 (not important to you or anyone else either) and worthwhile fun tends to be in box 1 or 3 (if you enjoy it, then it's probably important to you). But if you *can* enjoy the box 2 jobs that's a bonus, since you will increase the total amount of enjoyment in your life, as long as you always remember to keep the time spent in box 2 under control in order to spend plenty of time in box 3, the one that really matters.

Exercise:
Can you think of any jobs that you've spent longer on than you really needed to, for one of the following reasons?

- You thought it was important when really it was only urgent

- It was important to others, but not to you

- You wanted the job to be done to a higher standard than was really necessary

- It was fun to spend time on

These unimportant jobs will tempt you to spend too much time on them, at a cost to the ones that really matter. The ones that really matter can easily be neglected if they are not urgent; they are the box 3 tasks, which are examined next.

CATEGORY 3: IMPORTANT BUT NOT URGENT

This is the key box to a better life! Let me illustrate this.

Exercise:
Write down one thing that you could do today that would make your life better in the future.

You might have written training, reading, planning, thinking, spending time with family, etc. Whatever it was *will* have been *important* to you, but, because it was something that you don't *have to* do today, *non-urgent*: box 3! All prevention is in box 3 (treating symptoms is boxes 2 or 1). All self-development is in box 3.

Because most of us are by nature short-term thinkers and reactors to situations rather than planners, box 3 is the most easily neglected. Almost every box 1 problem could have been handled earlier as a box 3 problem, with much less stress.

Have another look at the list of box 1 problems used as examples in the earlier section:

- crisis in the factory
- safety hazard discovered
- angry customer demanding answers
- board report due by lunchtime
- problem with shipment just leaving
- teenage son held at police station.

Can you see how they could all have been avoided by box 3 activities like planning ahead, installing quality-control systems and taking time to communicate with your colleagues and team? In fact, by definition an urgent job was non-urgent at some time in the past. When would you rather tackle it?

This is what distinguishes good managers from floundering fire-fighters – if they are caught out by a box 1 problem, they ask themselves 'What can I do to stop that happening again?' and then they take the action. They are operating in box 3.

An example

Most jobs involve a certain amount of fire-fighting that cannot be predicted or prevented; indeed, it is part of the job. For example, a computer systems engineer's time may be divided between

- working on new developments
- responding to user problems and breakdowns
- routine maintenance.

Which boxes would you put these in?

New developments are probably box 3, user problems are probably in box 2, but what about routine maintenance? It is not urgent, it is a planning-ahead type activity (box 3), but it is probably not what the engineer regards as his/her reason for doing the job so it does not qualify for box 3; perhaps it's box 4, to plan in for later and to spend the minimum time on or delegate if possible. But surely maintenance is important.

This confusion is due to the difference between job description and personal goals which was discussed earlier. In terms of the job description all three of the above task types are important and are therefore box 1 (customer service) or box 3 (new developments and planned maintenance). But in terms of the engineers' personal work objectives, they may well feel that only the new developments deserve box 3 status, while the others are box 2 or 4, to be dealt with in the minimum effective time.

Job description		*Personal work objectives*	
1 Respond to user problems and break-downs	2	1	2 Respond to user problems and break-downs
3 New develop-ments Routine mainte-nance	4	3 New develop-ments	4 Routine mainte-nance

If in doubt, the engineers should allocate their time according to their *personal* objectives, which will also in the long run lead to more effective performance and results for the *company* . Plenty of new developments will be generated, while the engineer will still satisfy the maintenance and service requirements in the most time-effective way.

Fitting the box 3 jobs in

Even though they are important both to you and to the company, box 3 jobs are the first to be neglected, or procrastinated, because they don't 'shout for themselves'. Box 3 jobs should be planned into your diary system so that they are certain to get their share of your time. But if they are never urgent, when should they be done? It would certainly not be sensible to leave them until they become urgent enough to be a box 1 crisis!

The difficulty is that there will always be enough 'reasonably urgent' jobs to ensure that if you worked on jobs purely in order of *urgency* you would never reach the very *important* box 3 jobs. This means that you will need to jump the queue with some of the box 3 jobs, doing them anyway and making some fairly urgent jobs wait. This is not a problem as long as none of the box 2 jobs reach their deadline. (A detailed procedure for diary planning is given later in this chapter, and the next chapter deals fully with procrastination.)

So, you have tackled the occasional box 1 job (they are rare because you do plenty of box 3 planning ahead), you are despatching the box 2 jobs with the minimum of time and making sure that you fit in a good number of box 3 jobs since they are the key to keeping tomorrow under control and to making progress. You will find that there are some gaps when you have time to spare. Then, and only then, can you visit box 4.

CATEGORY 4: NOT URGENT, NOT IMPORTANT

Clearly these jobs should be at the bottom of the pile and should only be done when everything else is finished. In practice this means that they will perhaps never be done, and some textbooks say 'bin it' for this category. However, there are two exceptions. One is that, a bit like box 3 jobs, if these box 4 jobs are left *they may become urgent*, which will be worse for you (more stress, and less control over when you do them). For example:

- backing up computer files
- organizing office Christmas party
- filing
- car maintenance
- mowing lawn
- clearing leaves from roof gutter.

(If you find yourself thinking that some of these are important because if they are not done they could be costly, remember that the definition of importance is whether it contributes to your objectives. Although you do need to do these, you would delegate them if you could, or you would do them in the minimum time. They are therefore not important!)

So, although they are not important and never will be, it may be worth doing them sooner rather than later. So you could plan them in, while making sure that you spend only the minimum time on them.

The other exception to the 'bin it' rule is that box 4 jobs are often done for fun. In fact many fun things fit into this category. And some fun is essential if you are to be effective the rest of the time. As long as you know it's fun and are still keeping up with the other jobs in the other categories, then fun is OK. For example:

- playing on the computer
- doing the easy parts of your job that really should be delegated
- visiting customers whom you like
- chatting with work colleagues.

I know that you could put a case for any of these being important, but that would probably be rationalizing; you know they don't really need to be done, so you may as well admit that you are doing them purely for fun.

By the way, fun could well be one of your life objectives, and it can be found in all of the boxes, not just box 4.

FOUR TYPES OF FUN

1 Seize the moment	2 Enjoy the necessary tasks
3 Put time aside for quality-of-life pleasures	4 Relax and unwind

Fun in box 1

Living in the here and now, sometimes called 'taking time to smell the roses', is box 1 fun. For example, playing with your children and sitting looking at your garden with a glass of wine on a Sunday afternoon are perhaps the kind of activities that life is all about. They are therefore in box 1: do it now (or lose the moment) and take a good length of time to do it. This is true 'quality time', the reason for all the manoeuvrings of saying no, reducing time spent on other jobs, planning and delegating. What a shame to do all this and then at the last minute decide to watch TV (box 4) or write a letter to someone you don't really like (box 4) when you could be playing with your children! Imagine coming home tired after a hard day at work and being asked by your three-year-old son if you will play football with him. It would be easy to say 'Let's do it later, I just want to sit and read the paper for a bit first', but if you did this you would be choosing a box 4 activity instead of a box 1 activity – the ultimate crime! This is why defining your objectives is so very important. Without it you will not know clearly what is important and what isn't until it's too late.

Fun in box 2

If you cannot avoid doing tasks that are urgent, often for other people, you may as well enjoy them. Since about half your time is spent in box 2, enjoying it will have a big impact on your total enjoyment of life. In chapter 2 we saw how enjoying the price is important in helping you put in the box 3 work to achieve the results you want; similarly, any box 2 task can be enjoyable. Even dealing with a really unpleasant or aggressive person can be enjoyable if you set yourself a personal challenge to enjoy it: how polite and calm can you be? What can you learn from the situation? What questions can you ask them to throw them off guard (for example, 'Are you having a fun day?')?

Fun in box 3

This box doesn't have to be about planning every minute in your diary:

- 2.00   Arrive at beach
- 2.05   Deploy buckets and spades
- 2.30   Estimated completion of castle.

But if you put some time aside for important activities, as a big blank square in your diary, you then have the freedom to use that time in any detailed way you want. You have decided not to let any box 2 jobs intrude and not to let any box 4 jobs tempt you away from it. For example, you may allocate the whole of Saturday afternoon to playing with the children, or going for a walk with your partner, or going to the beach or visiting a friend. Exactly what you do does not have to be planned and can be as fun and spontaneous as you like. Planning your day does not rule out spontaneity!

Fun in box 4

Most people have a need to do something 'blank' occasionally, to unwind. If you don't have a box 3 activity to help you unwind (something like fishing, reading or making wooden toys might qualify), then being a couch potato is an alternative. But as you can see, the other three boxes have better types of fun, so it is best to keep this last box to a minimum.

Watching television is a particularly tempting activity which is probably in box 4 for you; have you noticed how it takes less than 30 seconds for you to get hooked and then afterwards you find yourself saying 'Why did I watch that?' Most TV-watching is a totally passive activity, requiring no input and no decisions from you, so it's an easy option to take. Whilst it does sometimes have educational aspects, the TV is probably the biggest time-waster in society today. You can illustrate this by asking yourself the question 'If I had only a week to live, how much of it would I spend watching TV?' You could also think about what you would do this week if your TV broke down. What could you do, this week, instead of watching TV?

A word of warning about box 4 jobs: sometimes they are hard to recognize and can be masquerading as types 1, 2 or 3. For example:

---

things you 'ought' to be doing:

- the gardening
- that extra work for the office
- decorating the spare bedroom
- reading the book which was given to you as a present

---

finishing what you wish you hadn't started:

- visiting a friend who you don't really like, simply out of politeness
- returning a visit or invitation
- the embroidery/kit car/shed/DIY project that was an impulse buy and is now taking ages
- 'I promised I'd do it, and even though it's turned out to be unpleasant I ought to finish it'

jobs for other people:

- helping them out when you know how to do something and they don't
- 'it's for a friend'
- 'it was hard to say no'
- 'they'd do the same for me'
- 'I need to stay well in with him'

All of the above *may* be important and you *may* have time for them, but they could also be box 4 jobs. Think carefully about whether they are *really* important to you. Are you only doing them because you'd feel guilty if you didn't? Are you doing them because someone else has made you feel that you should do them? If you had the choice, would you ideally not do them? If there were no adverse consequences if you left them, would you still do them? Are you throwing good time after bad?

My recommendation is that you cut your losses on these jobs. If you can't bring yourself actually to bin them, then put them to the bottom of the pile. If they involve other people you should be assertive and explain that you are not planning to allocate time to that job at the moment.

RISKS

Each box has risks associated with it.

Box 1: important and urgent

Box 1 has the risk that jobs will appear to be in it when really they are not important. Are you spending too much time on jobs that are really not that urgent or important? Too many false box 1 jobs could mean failing to achieve a real one! If you are spending more than 10 per cent of your time on box 1 tasks you need to plan ahead more.

Box 2: urgent but not important

Box 2 jobs tend to squeeze out box 3, and can be mistaken for important jobs just because they are urgent. Are you running around on urgent tasks at the cost of your important long-term goals? This box should never exceed 50 per cent of your time.

Box 3: important but not urgent

Box 3 jobs are the ones you will be prone to procrastinate, which will lead to too many box 1 jobs later. Are you procrastinating important tasks because you don't *need* to do them today? Are you using unimportant box 2 tasks as an excuse? Are you being tempted off course by box 4 activities? Aim to increase this box to at least 30 per cent of your day, preferably more. See the next chapter for ideas on how to reduce procrastination.

Box 4: not important or urgent

Box 4 jobs can be done for fun at the expense of categories 2 and 3, but the amount of time you spend on them could be a sign that you are letting other people's priorities overrule your own. Are you spending no more than 10 per cent of your day on box 4 jobs?

Aim for		
	10%	40%
	40%	10%

PLANNING THE FOUR TYPES OF TASK INTO YOUR DIARY

The procedure for doing this is as follows:

■ Do the box 1 jobs straight away.

■ Write into your diary the (box 2) urgent jobs, positioning them so that they are finished before the deadline with a reasonable safety margin. Allocate the minimum amount of time to them – remember, they are not really important.

■ Then fill about half of the gaps with box 3 jobs, which are more important.

1   block in a period of time when you will give each one some attention

2   make the blocks of time short, say 30 minutes to an hour, so that interruptions can usually be made to wait until afterwards

3   jealously guard this time against other people encroaching upon it.

You will need the other half of the gaps for taking care of the urgent jobs which have not yet appeared, but certainly will!

(You may need more than half of the gaps for problems which crop up; this depends on the nature of your job and on your previous history of doing or not doing box 3 tasks.)

■ Only once this is done and you find you have time to spare should you put in box 4 activities.

So if you had done eight things today, some from each category, they would probably look something like this:

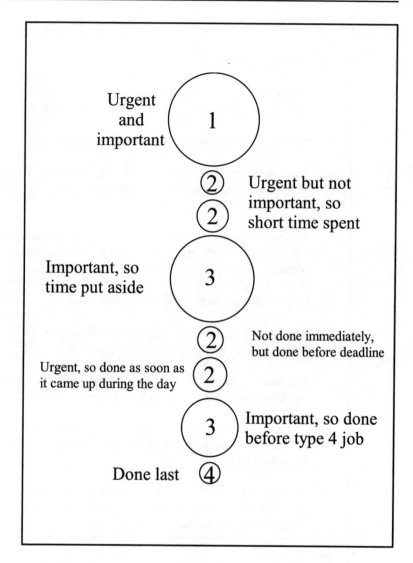

This diagram shows the jobs done in order, starting with the top one. The size of the circle is the amount of time you spent on it. The number is the category of the job (urgency and importance).

To finish this chapter, let's test this model. Here is a list of tasks, but which categories should they go in?

Exercise:
Categorize the following:

1 Your Chief Designer phones in sick, so this afternoon's meeting will have to be cancelled and everyone told.

2 Yesterday's production figures need to be analysed.

3 Your secretary's word processor has broken down, the systems technician is on holiday, but you happen to know how to re-boot from the systems disk.

4 You receive a sales report from your Sales Manager about the problems being encountered on a large potential new account.

5 Road traffic accident outside the office window.

6 Your boss requests next year's sales forecast – to be on his/her desk in a fortnight, preferably sooner.

7 The roof in the corner of the office has started leaking. Someone has put a bucket under it to catch the drips.

8 A quality problem has been discovered which could affect the last three weeks' output, some of which has already been dispatched.

9 Your secretary tells you that the Paint Shop Manager's wife left him last night and that 'he is not in much of a state'. You'll need to have a chat with him.

■ Answers:

1 Cancelling the meeting: certainly not deserving of any significant amount of time, but the urgency is harder to determine. It could probably wait an hour or two, but must be done at least 3 hours before the meeting, therefore box 2 (delegate or do quickly).

2   Analysing figures: in theory this would be an important job, and also fairly urgent since anything you discover could need urgent action (box 1). In reality though, this could be a routine task which you do without questioning it. If there is a serious problem you should know about it before reading it in the figures, either by 'MBWA' (management by wandering around) or by reports from supervisors. Many problems could not be diagnosed from just the figures alone, so this could well be box 4: 'don't!' You should consider scrapping the paperwork and doing more MBWA instead! If this is too radical to be feasible, then box 2: have a quick scan, or delegate with instructions to report anything significant.

3   Fixing word processors is unlikely to be high on your list of objectives in life, although being nice to your secretary could well affect your ability to achieve *other* objectives that *are* important. But this job is urgent to you because it is urgent to him/her, therefore box 2: do straight away but, unless impressing your secretary is important to you, spend the minimum time on it.

4   Sales problem report: clearly important, but urgency is difficult to assess. This job could probably wait a day or two, but not longer, so you should plan some time into your diary for the afternoon or tomorrow (box 3).

5   Road traffic accident: unless you are a doctor or an amateur first-aid enthusiast this is not important by our definition. (Ask yourself whether the motorway crash which killed eleven people should really have been the first item on the news; was it really the most important event shaping the future of our country that happened today?) However, it is most certainly urgent, and you should respond immediately by calling an ambulance and checking that first aid is being performed. Delegating this could be too risky: I would do it myself if the people available were less competent than me (this goes against the normal

principle of delegation, outlined later in this book, where delegation is recommended if they can do it at least 70 per cent as well as you), so box 2: do it now but spend the minimum time on it.

6   Request from boss: you have two weeks for this, so it is not urgent. But I would plan it into my diary so as not to forget it. Next year's sales forecast may not be important in itself, but keeping the boss happy is, since other important things depend on it. Collecting the figures would probably be delegated, but I would plan the timescale and reporting back into my diary with plenty of buffer time, to make sure it was under control with minimum stress (box 3).

7   Roof leak: not important or urgent. Delegate or ignore. However, it *would* be urgent if it was likely to get worse and *would* be important if customers were likely to see it, so box 4, but under some circumstances 2 or 3.

8   Quality problem: the only item on this list that is definitely in box 1. You need to get on to this right now, and take as long as is necessary to sort it out. By the way, what caused this box 1 item? Probably not enough time spent on earlier box 3 activities like quality control, good management, setting up systems, relationships with suppliers, etc.

9   Paint Shop Manager's wife: this item shows the difficulty of pigeonholing tasks. Perhaps you just need to make an appearance later and look sympathetic (box 4). Perhaps you need to nip down there right away, make the right noises and make a quick decision about whether he is fit for work (box 2). Perhaps you need to sit down with him later for some counselling, putting aside a good chunk of time and really helping him get sorted out (box 3). Perhaps you need to get down there now and do this, as your managers are your most important resource (box 1). Personally, I would choose box 1, but this depends on your own management style, which is a subject not for this book!

■ Conclusion:

Not all situations can be put into black and white boxes like this, but thinking about your objectives, and whether to plan a job in, delegate it or do it now, is a useful thought process to practise. You will then be controlling your time rather than responding and letting your surroundings and other people control you.

ACTION PLAN

■ Box 1: one activity that is important and urgent

Now think: is it *really* both of these?

■ Box 2: one urgent but unimportant job that I spent too much time on recently

■ Box 3: one non-urgent but important job that I will plan into my diary

■ Box 4: one non-urgent unimportant job that I do for fun

■ Box 4: one job that I only do because I feel I ought to, when really it is not important to me

I will bin this job!

Now, as we discussed earlier, start a job-planning system *today*.

- list all your current jobs to do
- assign each one an order of urgency and a measure of importance
- then, write these into your diary or day's plan, making sure that the unimportant ones are given minimal time and are done before their deadlines, while the important ones are given as much time as possible
- leave approximately half your day free for problems (box 2 jobs) which will crop up during the day
- you should have found between half an hour and two hours for your box 3 activities.

Make planning a habit: at the end of each day, plan the next one.

Generally you don't need to think 'Which box does this job go into' every time a problem lands on your desk, but you do need to think 'It may be urgent, but is it really important?' and you do need to think 'It's important so I'm going to make sure I find time for it, either today or planned into my diary for the future.'

Never lose sight of what's important and what isn't.

In the next chapter we will look at procrastination, which is the single biggest cause of failure to do those important box 3 jobs, and therefore of failure to achieve the objectives that you *want* to achieve and *can* achieve.

4 Procrastination: how can you beat it?

Your objective in this chapter is to find at least one method that you can use to beat procrastination. You may find several that you can use for different types of situation. At the end of the chapter you will be asked to make a note of the ones you have felt would work for you while reading this chapter.

We all put jobs off until another time, for a variety of reasons. Yours might be

- the job is too big to face
- the first part of the job is unpleasant
- the whole of the job is unpleasant
- there are too many tempting distractions
- you find it easier to do short-term or quick jobs instead
- you are not sure how to do it
- fear of unpleasant results if you fail
- lack of physical energy.

The results of procrastination are likely to be

- increased stress as you think about the task you are avoiding
- not spending time on the things in life that really matter
- not spending time on the tasks that will bring long-term results
- having to do things in a rush, therefore badly
- jobs becoming worse, harder to do, more expensive or more urgent
- time wasted on irrelevancies, so less achieved in total
- other people concluding that you are inefficient.

We need systems and methods which will help us overcome our natural tendency to take the easiest option at any given moment.

Exercise:
Here are twenty-five strategies you could use. After reading each one and applying it in your mind to the tasks that you are currently putting off, give it a mark out of ten for how useful it is to you.

1   Write a total list of every major job that you need to do and put it on the wall where you can see it. This will remind you about what is important and keep you focused on being productive.

■   How useful, out of ten, would this method be for you?

2   Have a look at your list and cross off the ones that really don't matter. Ask yourself whether they will matter in five years time if you don't do them. Could you live without them? Are you doing them out of a sense of duty rather than because you want to do them? If you can't bear to delete the job totally you could transfer it to a 'maybe someday' list where you would not feel guilty about it and where it would not interfere with more important tasks.

■   How useful, out of ten, would this be for your jobs list?

3   Break large jobs down into chunks. Using the example of painting a room, I might decide on Friday evening that *all I will do* tomorrow is decide on the colour, which is quite a fun job anyway. Next week, all I will do is go out and buy the paint – no problem, I can do that! Then, the week after (or maybe sooner) I will plan to paint just one wall. If you keep taking small steps in the right direction you can't fail to arrive, especially as momentum will probably take over and you may well accelerate. Also, having broken the job into chunks, you can plan these into your diary so that you know the completion date and can be confident that it will be achieved.

■   How useful, out of ten, would this method be for you?

4   Write a daily jobs-to-do list the evening before, so you commit yourself to doing some tasks the next day. Enjoy crossing the jobs off as you complete them. Write the list in order, mixing in the enjoyable jobs with the tough ones, and stick to the order.

■   How useful, out of ten, would this method be for you?

5   Put the unpleasant jobs (for example, the washing up or phone calls to difficult customers) at the top of your jobs-to-do list or make it a rule to do one unpleasant job at the start of the day, so that you can feel smug for the rest of the day.

■   How useful, out of ten, would this method be for you?

6   Make appointments with yourself in your diary, in order to keep times free to do certain important jobs. For example, you might set aside half an hour on Monday afternoon for writing your report, or allocate a Sunday in three weeks time to painting a room. Writing it down makes you much more likely actually to do it.

■   How useful, out of ten, would this method be for you?

7   Set yourself a deadline and declare it or promise it to someone else. Tell your boss they will have the report on their desk by Friday. Tell your visitors that when they come at the weekend they will be able to see the new patio, finished. Some people would not choose to have this extra stress, while others thrive on a challenge.

■   How useful, out of ten, would this method be for you?

8   Consider delegating the job or paying someone else to do it. You could pay an accountant to do your tax, which might save you money in the long run. It may cost you less than you think to pay a gardener to mow your lawn.

Or perhaps you could trade: is there someone who would enjoy this task or for whom you could do something else in exchange?

■ Could you use this method? Mark out of ten:

9   Have a fixed routine for when you do certain things; for example, always top up your oil on Saturday morning before breakfast, always wash up after eating or always spend half an hour writing letters on Thursday evening. We are creatures of habit, and habits make unpleasant tasks easier because we don't question them.

■ How useful, out of ten, would this method be for you?

10   Make sure you have a desk that encourages you to work. As well as making sure it is clear of junk (see chapter 10), you should do things like drinking coffee, chatting and reading the paper elsewhere so that when you return to your desk your subconscious equates 'desk' with 'work'. Have everything you need at your desk so you have no reason to get up and walk around.

■ How useful, out of ten, would this method be for you?

11   Measure your progress: keep a graph of progress (pages read, letters written this week, minutes spent exercising, etc.), ideally a cumulative graph showing 'actual' against 'target' so that if you have a bad day you can always catch up on the next day.

■ How useful, out of ten, would this method be for you?

12   Appoint a task-master to make you improve. Get a close friend to be your conscience and your reminder. Ask them to monitor your daily jobs list and to ask you at the start of each day (a telephone call would suffice if they do not live near) which of the jobs you intend to do, and whether you

did yesterday's jobs yesterday. Ask them to be strict with you and to accept no excuses. If you are using the self-talk process, you could ask them to check that you have remembered it. If you are intending to get your desk under control, you could arrange for them to check it once a week.

■ How useful, out of ten, would this method be for you?

13 Jolt your laziness: this method focuses on the consequences of not doing the job, in order to reduce your apathy: think about the worst that could happen, if you did nothing and the job became more serious. Paint a vivid, exaggerated picture in your imagination. Imagine those window frames that you should have been painting becoming rotten and crumbling and costing a fortune to replace. Imagine your unserviced car breaking down miles from anywhere on a dark night when it is raining and you are only wearing your best suit. Imagine that neglected customer complaining to your boss, or that sloppy employee causing a serious accident. Now, are you going to get the task done?

■ How useful, out of ten, would this method be for you?

14 Confront your fear: think of the worst that could happen, and realize that it's not that bad really. For example, when telephoning a difficult customer to ask for a repeat order ask yourself what is the worst that could happen? How likely is this scenario actually to take place? What actions can you take to make sure that it won't happen?

■ How useful, out of ten, would this method be for you?

15 Plunge in and get started: even if you don't have all the information or all the equipment, start the job anyway. The momentum will keep you going once you have started. For example, I find painting a room very enjoyable

once I have started, even though I have to stop to cover up the next bit of carpet, move objects out of the way or nip out to get more paint. The thing is to *start*. If I had to prepare fully before starting, I know I would never start. Similarly, with difficult phone calls, once you have made the first one the process becomes much easier, so the trick is to plan the approach of your calls generally and then dial the first number almost without thinking. As with all of these methods, different ones will work for different people: some people *need* plenty of preparation time, while others use it as an excuse.

■   How useful, out of ten, would this method be for you?

16   Leave the job out, somewhere visible. This could mean leaving the writing pad and pen out on the table for that difficult letter, or leaving the pile of bills to be paid on the table with the cheque book, or putting the tin of paint in the middle of the hall. Leaving books open makes starting to read them much easier. Leaving the tools out makes starting the repair job much easier. However, this method would only be used on one job at a time or your environment will get out of hand.

■   How useful, out of ten, would this method be for you?

17   Consciously choose your stress level for today. Do you want to have an uncomfortable day thinking about the jobs you ought to be doing but have not started, or do you want to have a good day having already done the tough jobs? Visualize both types of day. Now choose one.

■   How useful, out of ten, would this method be for you?

18   See the situation from the receiver's point of view. Your receiver might be your boss, your husband or wife, your children, visitors to your house, your subordinates or colleagues, or a customer. Ask yourself 'What will they think

if I don't do this job for ages, or deliver it late, or haven't done it by the time I next see them?' Do you want them to think this?

■ How useful, out of ten, would this method be for you?

19 See the task as an opportunity. This can be difficult, but is an interesting game in itself. The report for your boss is a chance to organize your thoughts, impress your boss and to get some ideas across and some changes made. Calling on a new customer could be a chance to make a new friend or to have a really interesting conversation, as well as a chance to make money. Any task can have a surprisingly positive outcome if you think hard enough about it. Can you think of any additional benefits for the tasks you are procrastinating?

■ How useful, out of ten, would this method be for you?

20 Visualize yourself taking action and completing the task easily, and enjoying it. Imagine yourself mowing the lawn and enjoying it, or visiting the difficult customer and receiving a friendly reception and a very large order. Has this positive picture made you keener to start?

■ How useful, out of ten, would this method be for you?

21 Focus on the successful result: undoubtedly the process of cleaning the bath is not fun, but the finished result, spotless and gleaming, will give you pleasure immediately as well as later when you slide down into it. Make the reason bigger than the price. In selling terms, focus on the order that you are certain to get if you make enough calls: what will you spend your commission on? Surely the holiday in Barbados is worth a few calls? You could combine this method with 19 and 20 above.

■ How useful, out of ten, would this method be for you?

22 Determine to enjoy the task as well as the result. Find something to savour in the process. For example, when stuck in a traffic jam you could examine and enjoy the details of the architecture above the shops, or the variety of the pedestrians. When sorting though your old files you could consciously enjoy throwing out-of-date memos into the bin. When you go to the supermarket you could make it a game to get the most miserable of the checkout operators to smile. When you mow the lawn you could make it a game to find the most efficient mowing pattern. If this was the *only* pleasure you got you would be a truly sad person, but since you've got to do the job you might as well enjoy it! If you can enjoy the process, then procrastination next time will be less of a problem.

■ How useful, out of ten, would this method be for you?

23 Reward yourself if you do a job that you were tempted to avoid; for example, after mowing the lawn give yourself a piece of chocolate. Link the reward to the task; for example, don't switch on the TV until you have written that letter, don't have a coffee until you have finished your report or telephoned that customer.

■ How useful, out of ten, would this method be for you?

24 Ensure that you have plenty of physical energy – lethargy can be a cause of procrastination. After work, do you find you can't be bothered to do anything? Do you need the weekend to recover from work? Do your children wear you out? The answer could be to take twenty minutes of exercise every other day, and you will feel more dynamic, more resilient, more decisive and more creative. And if you decide to, you can even enjoy the exercise too!

■ How useful, out of ten, would this method be for you?

25 Self-talk: say to yourself every day 'I love doing the tough jobs first', 'I start jobs straight away and finish them off without effort', 'I have nothing waiting to be done, so I am free to enjoy spending my time as I wish', 'My friends all think of me as dynamic and efficient'. Remind yourself to do this by putting a small notice or post-it note containing one of the above sentences on your bathroom mirror. Since your subconscious controls your behaviour, if you gradually reprogramme it by repeating these sentences every day you will find them becoming true: you will no longer be a procrastinator.

■ How useful, out of ten, would this method be for you?

Now, review the above list and the scores you have given to each one. Which are your preferred methods and how will you apply them?

Jobs I am currently putting off   *Method I will use to get them done*

1

2

3

4

5

5 *Time-wasters: can you reduce them?*

Time is a unique resource:

- you can't get more of it than your twenty-four hours a day
- you can't get it back once it's lost, however hard you work
- you only get to use your limited supply of it once
- this isn't the dress rehearsal, it's the real thing!

Don't waste it!

The objective of this chapter is to find out what your main time-wasters are and to give you some ideas on how to reduce them. Time-wasters are any activity that reduces the time you spend working on your goals.

The Pareto Principle states that 80 per cent of your results come from 20 per cent of your time. This means that the other 80 per cent of your time is used either on activities that do not produce results or on activities that produce results only very slowly. Could this 80 per cent be improved upon, or will 80 per cent always be wasted? Is the Pareto Principle an immutable law? Because if it is, there might be no point in trying to improve your use of time. The answer is that, yes, the Pareto principle *is* an immutable law, but it need not limit your output of results. Some people achieve a lot more than others, but their achievements still come from 20 per cent of their time. The reason for their improved rate of achievement is that the 20 per cent is used better and so is the 80 per cent. This is illustrated in the example below:

| | 'UNITS OF ACHIEVEMENT' | |
	High achiever	Underachiever
from top 20% of time	40	8 plus time wasted
from other 80% of time	10	2 plus time wasted
TOTAL ACHIEVED	50 with few time-wasters	10 plus lots of time wasted

But how can there be such a large difference between the two people's outputs? Surely time-wasters only represent the loss of a small fraction of the time in a day? The answer to this question lies in *how* the time is spent. Using the four-box model from chapter 3:

1 Urgent and important Crisis and vital jobs Do it now!	2 Urgent but unimportant Daily problems Spend minimum time on these.
3 Not urgent but important The key to all progress Plan and spend time on these.	4 Neither urgent nor important Avoid or do last, and in the minimum of time.

The high achiever and the underachiever would probably have been spending their time as follows:

High achiever		Underachiever	
10%	40%	15%	60%
40%	10%	5%	20%

The underachiever is spending more time in boxes two and four, where the time-wasters are all to be found, with the result that box 3 is neglected and box 1 jobs are more frequent. The high achiever (and remember that their achievements could be many things other than money or material gain) is spending *eight times as much time* in box 3, so their rate of achievement is massively multiplied. These numbers are only an example, but they do show how, starting with the same total amount of time, a small increase in the allocation of time to the wasted boxes (2 and 4) can dramatically reduce your results.

In the next section we will examine some of the commonest time-wasters that drag or tempt us into boxes 2 and 4, respectively.

Exercise: How many of the following apply to you? Time-wasters	1 Not a problem	2 Occasional problem	3 Problem worth addressing	4 Major problem: must be adressed
Beginning the day: 'warming-up time'				
Being too much of a perfectionist				
Chatting/drinking coffee				
Cluttered desk				
Distractions				
Doing all the detail yourself				
Doing irrelevant jobs while avoiding unpleasant ones				
Doing several jobs at once				
Having to correct your own mistakes				
Indecision and postponement				
Looking for things				
Parts of your job which do not contribute to your personal objectives				
Travel				
Unclear responsibilities and borderlines				
Walking from place to place				
Writing long reports				
Feeling tired at the end of the day				

Time-wasters	1	2	3	4
Chasing people who don't get back to you				
Correcting other people's mistakes				
Having to do other people's jobs				
Inaccurate information from others				
Inadequate resources				
Interruptions				
Irrelevant tasks for the boss				
Long telephone calls				
Meetings				
Playing telephone tag (each happens to be out when the other calls				
Reading long reports				
Talkative people				
Taking messages for people				
Task duplication with others				
Trying to find people				
Unclear objectives				
Untrained staff				
Waiting for people who are late				

Time-wasters	1	2	3	4
Others:				

The first table is a compilation of self-generated time-wasters. These are all within your control and are not someone else's fault. Many are box 4 activities: not important or urgent, but tempting. The general answer to these is better planning and more self-control.

The second table lists the time-wasters that are inflicted on you by other people, and these are more likely to be box 2 activities, although some might be box 4. The general answer to these is to focus on your own objectives and be assertive. Be determined to get the situation sorted out for next time. The next chapter deals in more detail with the subject of assertiveness and regaining control over other people's use of your time. If it is not possible to reduce how often these situations happen, then it may be possible to spend less time on them when they do arise.

Which type of time-waster was most common for you? Is your largest area for improvement that of self-discipline or your relations with others?

For many of the time-wasters listed, realizing that you have a problem is the first step towards doing something about it. If what to do is not then obvious, you can look up your particular time-wasters in the following table and get some ideas on what to do about them. The table is not designed to be read right through, but should be used to refer just to the sections that you need.

Beginning the day: 'warming-up' time	Always write a jobs-to-do list for each day the night before. This will ensure that you start your day with a focus on what is to be done. Also, if you have personal goals which excite you and if these work goals are at least fairly similar to your job description, you will feel motivated to get started. Your desk, which should be tidy and free from distractions, could also influence your motivation to start work.
Being too much of a perfectionist	Realize that you can't do everything perfectly, and that perfectionism is a recipe for stress and underachievement. Learn to do some jobs excellently and some jobs only as well as necessary. Chapter 3 explains when it is acceptable to do a job less well; only truly important jobs deserve the maximum amount of time, and there are not many of these. Chapter 9 examines personality drivers – including 'be perfect' – how they control your behaviour most of the time and what you can do to reduce their influence on you.
Chasing people who don't get back to you	It may be possible to arrange to meet them at a regular fixed time, so that a routine is established. If you arrange a meeting and you have reason to believe that they will fail to turn up, ask them to confirm that they will definitely be there. If necessary point out that they have been unreliable in the past. If they promise to get back to you with an answer, ask them when you can expect to hear from them and make a note in your diary to call them just after that date. If they are unable to give you a date, ask them when they will be able to. Sometimes it is possible to use 'If I don't hear from you I'll assume it's OK'.

Chatting/ drinking coffee	Some relaxation and socializing is essential – a major part of good management is understanding your people and knowing what is going on – but if you feel that time is being wasted on chatting you should first consider banning talking about yourself – you learn nothing new from this. Most people prefer to talk about themselves rather than hearing about you, so to be a good conversationalist you should learn to ask genuinely interested questions and to be a good listener. This allows you both to control the conversation and to learn. Get conversations back on track by saying 'Anyway, we need to agree . . ./sort out this . . .' Don't get involved in conversations that are not going anywhere, for example what was on TV last night, house prices, road works and traffic, or the terrible state of the organization/computer/boss. Walk away.
Cluttered desk	A major source of distractions and stress, desks are dealt with specifically in chapter 10. Some main points are that clutter encourages procrastination and stress, so it is important to work on only one major task at a time, to write every incoming job down for later action, to throw away as much as possible (into an intermediate box if necessary), to empty your in-tray every day and to make sure there are no piles of paper on your desk which have been there for more than a week: by this time you will be starting to forget what is at the bottom of them and they will be starting to put stress on you.

Correcting other people's mistakes	The first step is to understand the cause of the mistakes: ■ are they aware of the mistakes? ■ are they motivated to do a good job (understand the context and value of what they do, involved with the choice of method, etc.)? ■ are they competent and well trained? ■ could they or someone else check their work? ■ do they have the correct information?
Distractions	Consider changing the position of your desk or the direction it faces. Talk to your boss if you want larger changes made, explaining the problem. You may need to be assertive and explain to individuals that you would like them to change their way of working with you (the section in chapter 6 on interruptions may be applicable to your situation). Use a jobs-to-do list to help keep you focused. Daydreaming may be an essential part of your creative thought process. But if you feel that it is a problem, you could use the method of putting notices up to remind yourself of what your major goals are, what your jobs to do today are, and consider: 'Is this the best use of my time right now?'

Doing all the detail yourself	The first question is 'Why are you doing it?' If there are others to whom you could delegate but for various reasons you do not do so (for example they are already over-worked or would not be able to achieve the required level of quality), then you need to consider the importance of your objectives and the amount of time you currently have left to spend on them after doing this type of detail work. By coaching and involvement you can increase the amount that you can delegate to your team. (Delegation is covered fully in chapter 8.) If you have to do the detail yourself because you have no one to delegate to, the need to spend so much time on detail could be caused by your 'be perfect' driver (chapter 9), in which case you need to cultivate the ability to let go of jobs which are not important.
Doing irrelevant jobs while avoiding unpleasant ones	Procrastination is covered in detail in chapter 4, which suggests methods ranging from writing down your daily jobs to do in numbered order, to finding some objectives that are important and that you really *want* to work on.
Doing several jobs at once	This is probably caused by your 'hurry up' driver (chapter 9) and/or your personal organization system (chapter 10), which includes planning your diary, deciding what you will do each day and in which order and keeping to the list, and having a neat desk. Realize also that doing several jobs at once leads to increased stress and poorer results on all of the jobs.

Feeling tired at the end of the day	Are you taking enough exercise? Are you getting enough sleep? Are you working longer hours than necessary? Remember that working extra hours on a regular basis does not produce any more results, so you should take steps to reduce the hours. If this will create a problem with your boss, then see chapter 6 on how to discuss it with him/her.
Having to correct your own mistakes	If rushing is a cause of mistakes, you may need to read about the 'hurry up' personality driver in chapter 9. You could reconsider your prioritizing and allocation of time in order to make sure you spend enough time on the important things (chapter 3). You could analyse what your most common mistakes are and then start a system to prevent them. Some useful checklists are: what to pack, what is located where, what is filed under which subject, what to remember for certain events like giving talks, meetings, etc., whom to invite to which meeting, common mileages and times taken for journeys, etc. This avoids mistakes and avoids the need to think about a subject more than once.
Having to do other people's jobs	First decide whether you *want* to do the task or whether you would like the other person to do it. Then establish why they are not doing it: are they not capable, or are they using your time in order to free up their own? You can then plan whether to develop the person's skills in order to make them capable or whether you need to discuss with them their perception of their job role and yours.

Inaccurate information from others	Ask them where they got the inaccurate information from, and track it down to its source. This could be a person or recorded data (e.g. computer, written documents, phone list, etc.). Spend some time putting right the data for next time. Make it a rule to spend time putting right the *causes* of problems, not just the symptoms.
Inadequate resources	Lobby for these in a nice but persistent way, using phrases such as 'It would help me to be more efficient if I had these resources', 'Can you see it from my point of view?' Ask if they agree that the resources would help. Ask what action they will take to help you get them. Ask when the resources are likely to be available. If necessary, give your boss a note of what the resources would cost and what the savings would be. This will help him/her to justify the expenditure to the levels above them, and a note is much more difficult to ignore than a verbal request.
Indecision and postponement	Develop a personal action plan for procrastination, based on the ideas in chapter 4.
Interruptions	See chapter 6 for a full discussion of how to handle interruptions.
Irrelevant tasks for the boss	Clearly define your objectives with your boss. You can then ask him/her how much time they want you to give to any new tasks and which ones they want priority given to. This will make it more difficult for them to give you irrelevant tasks, and at least you will agree with them that these tasks only deserve to have minimal time spent on them.

Long telephone calls	Make all your phone calls in one batch. Make notes on what you want to discuss before you call. Keep conversations on track with 'Anyway, the reason I'm phoning you is . . .' or 'Anyway, what can I do for you?' Avoid talking about details with people who you are going to see soon. An answerphone also saves time since messages will tend to be brief and to the point.
Looking for things	Identify the most commonly misplaced items and then keep them in fixed places. Hang things on the wall where you can see them. If necessary, when buying items like scissors or keys get two or three of each, so you can have one in each place where you use them instead of moving them around and then losing them.
Meetings	For a full examination of meetings from a time-efficiency point of view, and what to do about bad ones, see chapter 7. If it is a meeting that you chair, ask yourself 'Is this meeting really necessary?' or 'Could I delegate this meeting, to be run by someone else?' Could parts of the agenda be delegated to a separate sub-group? If you have to have the meeting, make it more time-efficient (see chapter 7).

Parts of your job which do not contribute to your personal objectives	Clearly define your personal work objectives. If necessary, renegotiate your official job objectives with your boss in order to line them up as closely as possible with your personal ones. Any work done on job objectives which are not on your personal list is wasted, so it is important to get these off your job objectives where possible. Otherwise, spend as little time as possible on them. Is there someone else who would like to do them or who would benefit from doing them?
Playing telephone tag	Get an answerphone: it gives you control over when you talk to people, control over interruptions, and avoids 'telephone tag' – even if your messages become a conversation in themselves, progress can be made when you are both hard to contact. It has the added benefit that you know when they *haven't* called. If a machine is not feasible, you should leave a message saying when you will call again, or when you will be available for them to call you.
Reading long reports	If you have the authority you could return long reports, asking for a one-page summary. If you need to be more polite than this you could go and see the person and ask them to sum up the main points for you verbally. If reading the report is unavoidable, you could take it with you as a fill-in job when you are waiting for an appointment or when you arrive early. Marking key points with a highlighter pen is the most efficient way to read, because you are forced to concentrate and evaluate the information. Also, if you need reminding of the main points a second reading is then much faster.

Taking messages for people	You must always answer any telephone that is ringing and then take any messages, because it may be a customer. This is essential to your organization and therefore you must do it at all costs. But if you are regularly doing someone else's job and you feel that the trade in time is unfair, then you should talk to them, explaining how you feel. If they are not able to change their arrangements in order to cover the telephone more effectively you could perhaps try asking for something else in return: is there something they could do for you?
Talkative people	Start by saying how long you've got. Then keep conversations short by thinking about what you want from the discussion, keeping it on track with 'Anyway, what I want to ask you is . . .' or 'Anyway, what did you want to ask me?' Don't encourage them with open questions (apart from, if they are complaining, asking them what they are going to do about it), and halve the length of the conversation by not talking about yourself: recounting your own experiences teaches you nothing and allows them time to prepare their next speech. If the discussion is partly work-based you could prepare a handwritten list of items to discuss and use this as an informal agenda to show how many items are remaining and keep the pace moving. Also, if you meet people outside your office or working area, you can leave when the conversation starts to repeat itself or ceases to be useful. As a last resort, after you have made hints about lots of work to do, looked at your watch and shuffled your papers, you can tell them you are busy. Chapter 6 deals generally with assertiveness: how to ask someone politely if it is OK for you to be left to finish the job you are working on and to talk to them later.

Task duplication with others	First decide whether you want to do the task or whether you would like the other person to do it. Then agree clear guidelines with them or with your boss.
Travel	Pack a book in your briefcase, and another in the car, for fill-in reading when held up, since travel almost always involves waiting at the far end. Indeed it *should*, since allowing enough time to cover potential delays is advisable for low stress and punctuality. You could also consider travelling at times when most other people are not on the road: be different to the main rush. For the travel itself, you could try listening to educational tapes in the car or on headphones; the better tapes contain the information from many books condensed down into short form and can teach you about anything from selling skills to the meaning of life. If training tapes are new to you, I would recommend anything by Brian Tracy as a fascinating and informative start.
Trying to find people	Always arrange appointments before going to see anyone, and if they are unreliable consider telephoning first to check they have remembered (you could ask them if they are ready for you, or just let them know that you are on the way). Consider communicating by notes. If you need them more than they need you, then you are in a weak position. However, there is probably *something* that they want from you, in which case you could link this with what you want from them – get them to come and see you for what *they* want and they will be much more likely to keep the appointment. For example, offer to give them the cheque to pay the account at a meeting to discuss quality. Or arrange to sign forms for expenditure at a meeting where you also receive a project progress update.

Unclear objectives	Objective-setting starts with you: what do you want your job to consist of? It is then necessary to negotiate clear guidelines with your boss as to what objectives he/she wants you to work on. Although you may feel it is your boss's job to do this, you may need to help them do it, by initiating the objective-setting process.
Unclear responsibilities and borderlines	First decide whether *you* want to do the task or whether you would like the other person to do it. Then agree clear guidelines with them or with your boss.
Untrained staff	An important part of delegation is the skill of coaching your staff, in order that they can be able to do more for you (and themselves) in the future. (See chapter 8.)
Waiting for people who are late	Initially, read the 'emergency book' that you always have in your briefcase or car; but if someone makes a habit of keeping you waiting you have the following options: ■ take fill-in work, which could be important but non time-dependent ■ schedule meetings for earlier than you actually need them ■ keep *them* waiting occasionally ■ in conjunction with the above methods: take pleasure in predicting that the other person will be late – you are a step ahead of them! ■ explain that their regular lateness is not acceptable as you have a carefully planned day – use the four-step approach outlined in the next chapter.

Walking from place to place	This time-waster is difficult to avoid, since changing the layout of the building is not usually viable. But you could combine your trips into one, use the telephone more or use meetings more. A start would be to keep a log of all your trips so that you can pinpoint the main problem areas – they may not be as you expected.
Writing long reports	Write very short letters and memos. Use postcards or post-it notes. Never write more than one side of A4: no one will read it! Become expert with a word processor and spreadsheet, and learn to type using all of your fingers – this does not take long to learn and will make a difference for the rest of your life. For your own notes, develop a system of short abbreviations for common words, e.g. mtg = meeting, Eng = Engineer, sitn = situation, s'mkt = supermarket.

Finally, here are ten additional actions you can take to reduce time-wasters and save time.

1   Measure your time for a week: if you have the patience you should record your activities every 15 minutes, but you may prefer to do an approximate summary at the end of the morning and the afternoon, or perhaps just list all the time-wasters as they occur. Many people who try this are surprised to discover where their time really goes.

2   Develop a habit of reviewing each day at the end: was your time well used? To help you do this you could begin a learning diary, where instead of recording the events of the day as you would in a conventional diary, you record any or all of the following:

■   any new ideas that you have had
■   ideas you would like to spend more time thinking about
■   ideas that would like to discuss with others
■   questions that you would like to have answered
■   what you have learned that day
■   ideas on how to make progress towards your goals
■   time-wasters that you are planning to spend less time on

3   Think: 'What did I do today that was neither useful nor enjoyable?'

4   Give up TV. Most of what is broadcast is negative, or at best pointless. The best way I have found to reduce my TV watching is not to buy or look at listings of what is being broadcast. Within a few days you won't know what you're missing, and you won't care either.

5   Be very clear on what your priorities are each day: what are you going to do today that will really matter in a few months or even years time? What are you going to do today that is really important to you? Resolve to spend enough time on these tasks and to leave the rest until afterwards.

6   Beware of doing nothing, or fiddling around, while avoiding an unpleasant task.

7   Resolve to finish each job and put it away before starting the next one. This will prevent you flitting between them and finishing none of them, and it will also prevent you flitting between a fun task and an important one.

8   Question each routine job you do. Seriously consider 'If I was away for two months, who would do this job?' and then delegate it to them.

9   Realize that quality-of-life activities are not time-wasters and should be consciously savoured. For example, going for a stroll at lunchtime or sitting and looking at the sea does not achieve anything in itself, but it is not a time-waster if it increases the quality of your life.

10   Be assertive: don't spend time with people you don't like. It's *your* life, you get only one and it's too short to waste. You *can* control your time, even when other people are involved. In the next chapter we will look at how to do this.

6 Gaining control: the effect of other people on your time

People and *events* will dictate how you use your time if you let them. We saw in chapter 3 how most *tasks* or *events* are either not urgent or not important and can therefore be controlled. It is possible to reduce the time spent on unimportant tasks and plan for the important ones. Although you will still spend perhaps 50 per cent of your day responding to small unpredictable problems, the other 50 per cent is plenty to create results and achieve goals – remember that 80 per cent of your results come from only 20 per cent of your time.

People, on the other hand, can be much more tricky! In this chapter we will be looking in general at the idea of being assertive about how your time is used. It is yours to use as you see fit, and is not available for other people to use unless you choose to let them. We will look at interruptions, as a major category of other people affecting your efficient use of time. We will also be looking at ways to handle the various types of people who can be difficult to control or deal with.

The main sections of this chapter concern:

- assertiveness
- interruptions
- your boss
- friends and colleagues
- your team.

Your objective in this chapter is to consider the following:

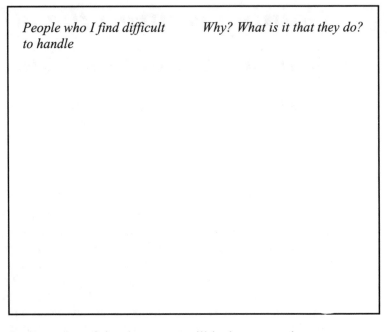

People who I find difficult to handle	*Why? What is it that they do?*

In the course of the chapter we will look at strategies you can use, so that at the end of the chapter you will be able to plan suitable actions for the above.

STRATEGY 1: ASSERTIVENESS

Assertiveness is not the same as aggression! The central principle of assertiveness is that *you* have rights but so do other people. Aggressive people forget the second part, while passive people do not assert the first part. In terms of time, you have a right to determine how you use yours and other people have a right to determine how they use theirs. Other people may feel that their time is more important than yours, or they may not even have considered the fact that you have other things you want to do apart from help *them*. With these people, assertiveness is required. The first step is to tell them, in a non-aggressive way.

If they want some of your time *right now*, you could ask them how long they need, because you are in the middle of something and you need to keep to your plan. If it's more than a couple of minutes, would they like to arrange a time to talk about it, maybe in an hour or two?

If they are asking you to do something for them, it is often useful to begin with some questions: when do they want it, why do they want it by then, how long are they expecting it to take you, and is it more important than any other thing you are doing for them?

If you decide that you are going to say no, you can then use the four-step process described next.

The four-step process for saying no

This can also be used to ask for what you want.

Step 1: I understand (but . . .). Explain that you understand their point of view (and make sure that you have, if necessary, asked plenty of questions in order to do so). You need really, genuinely, to understand their view, not just dismiss it with an 'I know but . . .' This may take some mental effort, but is a good way to gain some time while you think about how to express how you feel and what you are going to ask for.

Step 2: I feel. To say how you feel is not an easy thing to do, especially for those who have a 'be strong' driver (see chapter 9). It may require some thinking ('How *do* I really feel?'). The fact that it is rare for people to express feelings makes it all the more powerful.

Step 3: I want. Say what you want (probably to say no, but possibly to have more time, to have help or resources, to be paid for your time, or to have more warning next time). If you want to refuse, make sure you actually use the word no somewhere in the sentence; this has much more impact. If you have a complaint, then what you want should be more than just to let off steam – it should be to be given something in return.

Step 4: Check OK. Check whether they can see your point of view. Find out their reaction to the feelings and wishes that you have expressed. If they agree to your request, you have succeeded. If they disagree, listen to their reasons – they may be valid! If you then wish to persist or make a modified request in the light of what you now know, you can go back to step 1 and repeat the four steps.

This simple process contains all of the key aspects of assertiveness: respecting the views of others, expressing your feelings, asking for what you want and asking others for their views. Keep the order of the steps exactly as shown or their effectiveness will be greatly diminished. The power of this process comes from the fact that the middle two steps are the relatively aggressive ones but they are sandwiched between the nice considerate opening and the nice considerate closing, so you can get away with quite a powerful punch in the middle. Also, step 4 is linked to step 2, so if they say 'No I don't want to agree to that' they are effectively saying they don't care about your feelings, which you expressed in step 2. You have a right to have feelings, and if they acknowledge those then you are most of the way to success.

Vary the words to fit whatever feels natural to you. Here are some examples:

- 'Thanks for asking me to play on the team. I know you need someone and it's an important match, but I feel I've been neglecting my family recently and I want to spend the day with them, so the answer has got to be no, I'm afraid – can you understand that?'
- 'I know it's easy for me to do this work for you, and you probably think I'm really miserable for refusing, but I do feel that it's *your* job and that *you* should learn how to do it, so I'll teach you how to use the computer instead of actually doing the job for you – does that make sense?'
- 'I know how you love seeing the kids when you visit, but I feel that we need some quiet time, just as a family without any visitors, so would it be OK if we postponed your visit for a month?'
- 'I probably don't seem very busy at the moment, and I like chatting, but I'm feeling a bit snowed under at the moment and I wonder if we could meet later after I've finished this job. Is that OK?'
- 'I expect you think it's easy for me to do this job for you, but in fact the work I do for you is putting quite a burden on my other work, some of which earns me money, so I'm afraid that from now on I'll have to ask you to pay me for it. Does that sound fair?'

I recommend being very polite and unemotional at all times, and using open body language such as arms open, palms upwards. Potentially weak phrases like 'I'm sorry but . . .' or 'I'm afraid . . .' are OK because the rest of the process is so powerful – you are saying how you feel and asking for what you want, so there is no risk that you will appear weak.

It is important to use feelings rather than facts, because the other person cannot argue with your feelings. If you use facts they may argue, or have an answer that is logical but not what you want. In the first example above, if I'd said I was unable to play because of visitors they might have said 'Bring them along too' or 'They can babysit while you are out playing'; but they cannot counter my 'I feel I've been neglecting my family' with 'No, you don't'. If they counter it with 'No, you haven't' I can say 'Well *I* feel I have'.

If the whole process feels difficult, you can practice one step at a time. For example, you can use step 4 after making a request, or use step 1 as an introduction to how you feel about something.

Although this process is extremely powerful, it is not 100 per cent guaranteed. It relies on the other person being reasonably logical and wanting a good long-term working relationship with you. It will not necessarily work on a spoiled child or their adult equivalent. It will also probably not work on someone who is mugging you in a dark alley (you may want to consider what the four-step script would sound like!). However, in borderline situations like handling a difficult customer it has a good chance of being successful. For example, if you have (again!) been kept waiting for an hour to see a regular customer:

■ 'I understand that you are busy and that unexpected problems often come up, and I'm grateful for the time that you have given me, but it makes my life very difficult to organize if you sometimes keep me waiting for long periods. It would help me a great deal if you could keep reasonably close to the appointments that we arrange. Do you think that's a reasonable request?'

(If the reply is 'No, my days are too complicated' you can try 'Well, can you see it from my point of view?')

Certainly, being passive will have no chance of working, and being aggressive is only likely to work with a risk of problems in the future. The assertive method will always be your best option.

STRATEGY 2: RESIST INTERRUPTIONS

Interruptions do more than just lose a few minutes of your time on someone else's priority: they break your concentration, they give you a chance to procrastinate and slip into a box 4 unimportant job, and they add to your stress because while you are handling the interruption you are still thinking about the job you were in the middle of. You will handle the situation less well because you were not prepared for it and could not plan for it. The following are some actions you might take to reduce the frequency and duration of interruptions.

Make yourself harder to interrupt

Put a sign on your door. 'Do not disturb' is not enough, since you surely want to know about the *really* urgent problems and each interrupter may feel that theirs is urgent enough. Your sign should give the reason for your not wanting to be disturbed and the finish time. For example:

Please do not disturb.

Writing my monthly report until 3.30.

Thanks

Train your regular colleagues to respect your notices, by asking interrupters 'Can it wait until after 3.30, because I'm writing my report?'

If you work in an open plan office, you could put the notice on the back of your chair, or on a string across the entrance to your work area, or on a chair blocking the way into your work area. Some companies have signalling conventions, like a paper cup on the computer terminal meaning 'I am in the middle of writing a complex program'. You could discuss these ideas with your colleagues and agree a system.

Rearrange your desk so that your line of sight does not face out to the corridor but is sideways to it. This means that passers-by cannot easily catch your eye, but will have to come in and tap you on the shoulder. They will be much more reluctant to interrupt you if they have to do this.

Assign certain times of day as 'open hours' or 'do not disturb times' and publicize these.

As a last resort, hide. This would mean working in a spare conference room for an hour or two. It's not a strategy you could use regularly or you will be discovered and sought out, and it is not good if you are nowhere to be found when there is a genuine crisis, but it does make the point that you are working on something important and that only vital interruptions are allowed.

Stop them before they start

If someone asks if you've got a minute say politely 'No, not at the moment, but I could do it later if you like.'

Suggest an appointment to discuss it properly, perhaps after you have had time to prepare it, at a later specified time.

Hold a short daily meeting (perhaps only ten minutes) with your major interrupters, so that you can get everything out of the way in one hit. Most problems can then wait until the next meeting.

Think: 'Why did that interruption happen, and what can I do to prevent it happening again.' Look for patterns.

Be assertive: explain that although you like talking to them their interruptions are affecting your work. Ask if it's OK and whether they can see what you mean, because you don't want them to take your resistance personally.

Reduce their duration

Establish a time limit for the interruption at the start. This is good manners, means they know where they stand and can plan the pace of their talking, and makes the point that your time is valuable.

Remove extra chairs from your working area, perhaps leaving just one uncomfortable or wobbly one.

Stand up to talk to them. Gradually edge them to the door when you are ready to finish.

Use the word 'anyway' to keep the conversation on track: 'Anyway, has that answered your question?' or 'Anyway, I must get back to this report now . . .'

Meet unwanted visitors outside your office, in reception, in a neutral room or at their office, so you are free to leave when ready. Use 'anyway' to escape.

When agreeing to an interruption, write it down to signal that the interruption has finished, and to ensure that your mind is free to focus back on the job that was interrupted.

Action plan:
Which of the above methods will you use?

The next three strategies are aimed at your major interactions: upwards, downwards and across.

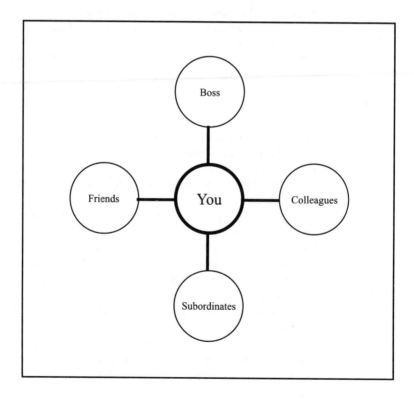

Each of the above relationships will need different approaches, as outlined next.

STRATEGY 3: TRAIN YOUR BOSS

Your boss is your most important customer, so a good relationship and top-class service are important. You must give your boss what he or she wants. However, you do have the ability to influence the relationship even though you are not in charge, and you can therefore take responsibility for getting it right. Here are some strategies that you might consider.

Clear objectives

Agree your job objectives with your boss, making sure that they are goals that are reasonably close to your personal work goals (see chapter 2). This will involve writing a list of what you feel are your work objectives, in order of priority, and showing this list to your boss for comments. Once you have this list, agreed by your boss, you can then make sure that as well as working on your personal priorities you can be careful not to neglect any areas which are viewed as particularly important by your boss.

Commit yourself to your objectives

Your list of work objectives should have timescales (with sub-stages if necessary), it should have measurable results (and this means a number that can be put on a graph) and it should include personal development activities for yourself and personal development activities for your team members. As with setting your personal goals, this process is uncomfortable because there is a risk you will fail to achieve some of them – but without it you will almost certainly fail to satisfy your boss.

Filter new tasks

Any new tasks which are given to you can be compared with the existing list; you can then ask and find out how important they are relative to the others, and make sure you understand fully where they fit in.

Avoid long hours

The best way to measure the contribution of an individual is achievement of results, but this can be difficult and in many organizations it is *effort* that is measured instead. A commonly used way to get a rough measure of effort is to look at the hours someone works. However, extra hours do not necessarily mean more is achieved, and if you have a busy life outside work you may resent the pressure to work long hours. If this is the culture in your organization it is important that you tackle it somehow and I would recommend a straight talk with your boss. Explain that you have an active life outside work which you feel is important and which you feel will keep you fresh and creative for your working time. Use the fact that your progress towards your agreed objectives is measurable to establish whether your performance is acceptable. Explain that you want to work hard and achieve results, and to be measured by this rather than the hours you work. Ask if they feel that this is reasonable. Surely this strategy is more acceptable to you, and to your boss, than your wasting extra hours at work purely because it is politically necessary to do so.

Obtain feedback

Ask your boss to give you feedback on your performance: is he or she happy, and how can you improve? Again, asking for feedback is uncomfortable since it is inviting criticism, but without it you cannot improve. Also, it is a good idea to detect problems with your performance (as perceived by your boss) as soon as possible rather than when it is too late. Feedback is also the first step towards being thanked.

Obtain thanks

Make sure your boss thanks you when you have done well. If you are one of the many who hardly ever receive praise or thanks, you should consider helping your boss to do it. Ask if the result on a certain task is satisfactory? If yes, ask if you did OK on it? If yes, say 'Thanks for saying so, it makes all the difference to be told that'. If they fail to get the hint after you have done this two or three times, you could be more open and ask if your performance is generally OK, and, if yes, ask if he or she could tell you when you've done something well as it motivates you and makes a difference to you. This is a reasonable request that is unlikely to be refused, particularly as most bosses *think* that they are already good at thanking.

Request information

Improve your motivation and your knowledge by training your boss to involve you more, initially by asking to know what's going on. You could ask for a weekly ten-minute communication meeting where they tell you what's happening at their level of the organization. It's a reasonable request, isn't it?

Learn from coaching

Arrange to be coached in areas where you lack knowledge or skills, by asking for a regular meeting to discuss the approach you are planning to take on a problem, to check that it is the best way and to make sure you are going in the right direction. This will enable you to learn from them, and will ensure that you achieve the best possible results.

Seek involvement in decisions

Ask to be involved in the discussions preceding major decisions, either just to sit in and learn or to have a say. After all, you can probably contribute something useful. This is a reasonable request, and is for the good of both the organization and yourself.

Manage the delegation process

If you want more responsibility (a personal choice) you can ask your boss to delegate work to you, and also, if necessary, you can help him or her to delegate it properly. For example:

- you can ask for the task to be written down clearly
- you can arrange to meet weekly or monthly to discuss progress
- in the event of interference you can explain that you want to try it your way (since after all it was delegated to you) because that is the only way you can learn to be responsible for it
- you can ask to review the task with your boss after it is completed, in order to learn (and get any deserved praise).

Request autonomy, gradually

Again, if you want more responsibility you can encourage your boss gradually to release control to you, by asking whether it is OK for you to do some tasks without having to check first – you have shown yourself to be reliable and this will save you both time. You will still be reporting afterwards to keep him or her informed. Then, later, you can suggest that rather than reporting every time you could just give them a monthly summary of what you have done.

An example of this would be authority for expenditure up to a certain limit: rather than having to check first, you could ask to be allowed to make the necessary decisions as long as you keep your boss informed afterwards. Once this arrangement has been working successfully for a while you can suggest that the reporting is reduced to a monthly summary in order to save time for you both. This way you are gradually increasing your autonomy, whilst reducing the number of interruptions and decisions for your boss.

Keep meetings brief but frequent

Train your boss to respect your time by setting a good example. Always ask if it is OK to interrupt them, say what you want to talk to them about, and ask how much time they can give you. Keep reports brief, either verbal with the key points as seen from their point of view or in writing on one sheet of A4 only. Spend the right amount of time with your boss – not too much, so you become a pest, but not too little so they feel they have no control and the relationship becomes awkward when you do meet. The right amount of one-to-one time will vary according to circumstances, but personally I would aim for either five minutes every day or half an hour once a week.

Define priorities clearly

Train your boss to respect your time by being politely assertive; for example, if asked to attend a regular but unconstructive meeting, you could suggest that the meeting is not the best use of your time because your contribution is minimal; you would rather be working on one of the important objectives that is on your jointly agreed list. To preclude the answer of 'I want you to do both' you might ask: 'Do you agree that the more time I spend on the top objective the better?' Similarly, if your boss asks you to do something that you feel is not a good use of your time because it is not important, you could ask: 'How important is it compared to such and such a job? How much of my time do you feel I should spend on it, roughly?'

Action plan:
What actions will you be taking to improve the working
relationship with your boss?

STRATEGY 4: NEGOTIATE WITH FRIENDS AND COLLEAGUES

A negotiation is a situation where you each have something the
other person wants and neither of you has all of the power. Working
with others in a team or with a colleague is often therefore a negotiation, although it is not often recognized as such. In logical terms
you should spend the minimum time helping someone else if their
objectives do not coincide with yours, but of course this would not
be acceptable team behaviour and also you will probably derive
pleasure (one of your objectives?) from helping someone else.
Helping others achieve their objectives makes them more likely to
help you achieve yours. If you have different skills and abilities
then you can help each other and a win/win situation results.

In situations where you *are* negotiating, not necessarily for
money but for someone else's time and effort in exchange for your
own, you should follow the sequence shown in the following diagram. The objective is to find a solution that is acceptable to them
and as beneficial as possible to you, and to make sure that someone
who is pushy does not end up with an arrangement that is disadvan-
tageous to you.

■ **Preamble**

Discover what is important to them. Ask questions and listen.	'How is it going?' 'Any problems?' 'Anything you need?'

■ **Get them to open first**

Mention the subject that you want to discuss, and ask what they can offer.	'By how much do you reckon you could reduce the waste?' 'What's the best delivery you can achieve?' 'How quickly could you do it for me?' 'How much time could you spare for this?'

■ **You open second**

If their offer is low, ask for what you want plus a bit. If it is high you can still ask for more.	'No, unfortunately that's not enough: I need at least a 10 per cent reduction/delivery within three weeks, etc.' 'Ideally you'd lend me someone to work on this over the weekend. Would that be possible?' 'Could you get it to me any earlier?' 'What I'm looking for ideally would be . . .' 'How close to this could you get?'

■ Trade

Use the format 'If you ... then I ...'	'If you could guarantee three weeks I could afford to pay for two days of overtime.' 'If you could finish it by Tuesday it would mean I could help you with ...' 'If you could lend me a person to work on this, I would have time to help you with ...'

Of course, not every interaction should be a negotiation, but if you think about it you will be surprised at how often you are negotiating. Sometimes a short-term lose/win can be justified in terms of the longer-term picture: relationships, helping others, and the good of the organization as a whole. The key is to make sure you are not in a *long-term* lose/win situation with anyone. Let's look at some of the interactions which can result in a permanent lose/win if not handled effectively.

'Wooden leg'

These are the people who avoid some tasks, and pass them on to you, by saying that they 'can't do numbers' or are 'hopeless with computers', or say 'you're much better than me at handling difficult customers'. There is also sometimes an undertone of 'It's all right for you' which makes helping them particularly unrewarding. The best response is to ask whether they would like to improve in that area, and then ask what actions they are planning to take in order to do something about it. If appropriate, you might offer to teach them, so they can do it on their own next time.

'Kick me'

These people point out their own failings by saying 'Look what I've done now' or 'I'm always doing that', with the intention of being told by others they are OK, whilst getting others to carry the workload for them. An example might be 'Sorry I'm late again, I always seem to have trouble with the car when there's an important meeting on.' The answer is *not* to say 'That's OK, it doesn't matter' but to ask them what they want you to say. Then, after an embarrassed pause of suitable length, ask them what plans they have for doing something about it, since presumably they *do* want to improve the situation for next time.

The interrupter

This is the friend or colleague who arrives unannounced or at very short notice, expecting you to stop whatever you are doing in order to help them or expecting you to fit in with their plans. As we have seen earlier, the options are to use methods to make it harder for them to interrupt, to use methods to make the interruption as short as possible, or to be assertive and tell them that the interruptions are a problem.

The chatter

Start by defining how long you've got, and use an agenda of points to be covered with how much time is allocated to each point. Get their agreement at the start to keep to the schedule. Use the word 'anyway' to get the conversation back on track. As a last resort, escape by leaving the room with 'Oh look, is that the time, I must be off, I'll catch up with you later'. Consider communicating mostly by written notes. Make maximum use of answermachines, both yours and theirs if they have one.

The asker for help and advice

These people may honestly need your help, or they may just be lazy. They may be good at using flattery to get you to do their work for them. The important first step is to decide what your objective is. Do you want to spend time helping this person? If no, say no (see earlier) or refer them to someone else who you feel is better qualified to help them than you are. Always remember that you have your own objectives, which are important.

The patronizer

This person tells you what you already know, or talks about what they want to talk about, not what you are trying to ask. You can use

their ego to your own advantage by flattering them and asking them
to do work for you because they are so capable, they are the best
person. Load them up with work. Assume that they are making
good progress and be amazed if they have had problems. Learn to
enjoy dealing with them, where you used to find them annoying.

Action plan:
What actions will you be taking to improve the time
relationship with your friends and colleagues?

STRATEGY 5: EMPOWER YOUR SUBORDINATES

From the *time* point of view the main objective with subordinates is
to delegate as much as possible. This will develop them and also
free up your own time for the important tasks which cannot be delegated. Chapter 8 describes fully who you can delegate to, and how
to move everyone gradually into the competent and motivated category where you can then delegate to them. There is a short-term
price in the extra time needed for training, supporting and involving
which is worth paying in order to gain the long-term reward of
freedom from detail. But, once free, what are these important tasks
that you should spend your time on? Surely there will be nothing
left to do?

Ideally you will have every job delegated in order to spend your
time on leadership, which consists of the following four areas of
activity:

■ monitoring progress of *tasks* and taking corrective action if necessary
■ ensuring that all of the *individuals* are clear on the task, skilled, and
motivated

■ ensuring that the *team* is functioning well collectively
■ standing back and taking a *longer-term* view, choosing direction, and planning how to get there.

How much of your time could you save by delegating more, how much time do you use on truly unavoidable tasks, and how much is left for the above four leadership areas?

Daily tasks I could delegate if I had to		%
Daily tasks I could delegate if I had the right people		%
Routine tasks that I will never be able to delegate		%
Monitoring progress of tasks	%	
Individuals	%	
Team	%	
Vision and planning	%	
TOTAL LEADERSHIP TIME	%	
TOTAL OF YOUR TIME		100%

The top two categories are the ones to work on first. Try to delegate everything you can, and develop your staff so that they can do more. In chapter 8 we will look in detail at how to develop your team members into people you can delegate important work to.

The division of time between the four leadership areas is less important, as long as none of them is neglected. A distribution of 30–30–10–30 would be a good target to aim for, if you feel you need one. (I have only allocated 10 per cent of your time to team-building activities like problem-solving discussions, because although these are just as important as the other areas they tend to be more time-effective and therefore need less time than working with individuals on the monitoring of tasks or on their personal motivation and coaching).

An example

Everyone has a different job, a different team, a different organizational culture and a different personality, but as a rough approximation I would like to show an ideal working day with the many small activities gathered together into blocks to make the picture simpler to see. You may want to change the order, or the size of the blocks, and obviously each day will not be the same, but the example that follows should give a feel for what *being in control* would be like. The activities would be the same for a first-line supervisor, a senior director, a technical manager, a factory manager or an office manager. As you read it, think 'Is this me? Would this work for me? *Could* it be me if I had a really good team and delegated everything? How should I start to move towards this?'

1 hour	Walk round	Get a feel for what is happening Make sure that all individuals are OK Check on progress of key tasks that have been delegated
½ hour	Think and plan	As a result of the above, think and plan tasks and future development of individuals
½ hour	Read mail and reply	Empty in-tray Make decisions on all incoming items Plan delegation
¾ hour	Meet with team	Discuss progress, solve problems, communicate news and plans, jointly work on projects

¼ hour	Meet with boss	Discuss progress, synchronize priorities, obtain feedback and information on the wider picture
½ hour	Think and plan	As a result of the above, think about projects, consider implications for customers or colleagues
½ hour	Customers and suppliers	Ensure that relationships are good, gain advance warning of changes or problems, make joint plans
¾ hour	Lunch	Taken away from the office Possibly exercise or fresh air
½ hour	Self-development	Reading, learning, training
½ hour	One-to-one time with subordinate A	Two colleagues per day:
½ hour	One-to-one time with subordinate B	discuss progress, set goals, get to know them, motivate them, coach or involve them, delegate new tasks and explain

1 hour	Meet with colleagues	One to one or as group meeting: Communicate, solve problems and plan ahead
½ hour	Think and plan	As a result of the above, plan future actions and tasks that will need to be delegated
½ hour	Walk round	Evaluate progress made during the day, ensure that everything is prepared for evening shift if there is one
5 minutes	Plan next day	Write jobs-to-do list Tidy desk Leave office on time, only staying late if there is a really important crisis

A critic might ask: 'Is this person actually doing anything? It looks as if the area they manage could happily cope without them!' The answer is that it could, for a while, because all of the day-to-day tasks have been delegated. But, like a supertanker whose captain has jumped ship, although there will not be an instant disaster the organization will, without proper management, gradually drift off course and head for disaster. The manager is providing the long-term vision and strategy, he or she is anticipating the problems, finding out what the customers want and making sure that they get it, monitoring the key tasks closely and making sure the individuals and team are working in an efficient way to achieve them, and is also taking time out to think creatively. This is infinitely more valuable than looking busy by working on visible tasks that should really be delegated.

ACTION PLANS

Please mark on the lines below where you feel you are.

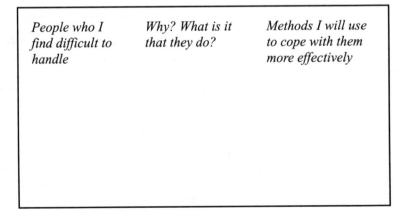

Now complete the table that you started at the beginning of this chapter:

People who I find difficult to handle	Why? What is it that they do?	Methods I will use to cope with them more effectively

7 *Meetings: power or peril?*

Meetings have a well-earned reputation for being time-wasters, and this is a great shame as a well-run meeting can be very powerful. Meetings can be the most time-efficient way to communicate information to a number of people, to motivate a team or to solve a problem. In this chapter we will look at meetings purely from a time management point of view – how to keep the time taken under control and how to get the maximum results from the shortest time. The chapter will be structured as follows:

- types of meeting and how they differ
- if you are chairing the meeting
- if you are not chairing the meeting
- types of people at meetings and how best to use their potential to contribute.

TYPES OF MEETING

Different meetings have different objectives and therefore need different handling. The main types are as follows:

- communication
- problem solving
- progress monitoring
- team.

There are key points to remember with each.

Communication meetings

Invite everyone who may be affected by the subject matter. This could be everyone who reports to you, or perhaps the whole company!

Don't let nerves, costs or logistical problems (e.g. 'Who will answer the phones during the meeting?') prevent you from inviting all of the relevant people – communication is vitally important and this type of meeting will pay dividends.

Use visual aids if possible, and provide a written note of the main points for participants to take away.

Allow time for questions at the end. If there are none, this could be because people are intimidated by speaking in front of others, so you could then move into an informal session where individuals can come up to you and ask questions.

Problem-solving meetings

Focus clearly on the problem at the start. Explain why it is important to those present, and describe the finished result that you would like to achieve (for example, to come up with a plan including names and dates, or to decide which machine will make which job, or to allocate areas in a way that everyone is happy with).

Invite everyone who will have to carry out the plan, but not everyone who will be affected by it – if you have more than about seven people the meeting will become too slow.

Make notes of actions, including details of who will do them and when they will expect to have results to report. Read these actions back at the end to check that everyone is clear and happy with them, and then circulate them within twenty-four hours as brief minutes.

Progress-monitoring meetings

This meeting should be action-driven, and will need to involve anyone who had an action at the last meeting. Ideally, progress of the project will be visible on some kind of chart, with names and dates clearly shown.

Each action must be apportioned to only one person, although others can be asked to support. Actions for people who are not present (person A) should be given to someone who is (person B). It is B's job to ensure that A does the action and if necessary comes to the next meeting to report.

Those not regularly receiving actions should be freed of the need to come to the meeting, but can continue to receive the minutes – smaller meetings will make faster decisions and build a closer team.

The meeting should be short, fairly formal and the members should feel under some pressure to have made progress so that the date of the next meeting puts some pressure on them to ensure results. If large problems crop up it may be necessary to arrange a separate meeting, perhaps of a sub-team, to avoid the progress meeting getting bogged down and developing a reputation for being long or boring.

Team meetings

A regular team meeting is absolutely essential to any management team. Do you attend one for the team that you are part of? Do you run one for the team that reports to you? Make sure the answer to both of these questions is 'Yes'!

The purpose of this meeting is to make the team *feel* like a team. This means being in the same room together at least once a week. Less often will not be enough. If the team members work different hours or in different locations, then they will have to come in especially: this meeting is too important to neglect for logistical reasons.

The meeting should happen at the same time each week, without fail, and anyone not attending should give you a very good reason in advance. If people are absent, the meeting should still go ahead.

The meeting can be combined with progress monitoring, problem solving or communication. The basic format should be that each person (including you) has five to ten minutes to say what they are working on, what events of significance have happened in their area, what problems they could do with help on, and what they expect to happen in the coming week. You can take the opportunity to ask them whether they have made progress on the areas that you are particularly interested in, and ask them for expected dates.

The tone of the meeting should be informal and friendly. Everyone should feel free to say what they like, even if it means admitting failure. Praise or thanks should be given to everyone at the meeting. Any reprimands should be kept for private talks later. Minutes should be brief, informal, produced by you, and list agreed actions and brief progress reports only.

WHEN CHAIRING MEETINGS

Prune

Could the size of the meeting be reduced? Regular meetings gradually get larger and longer; they never get smaller or finish of their own accord. Therefore, like a gardener, you need to prune the oversize meetings, pull out the ones that are past their prime, and start fresh new ones when required. Question the need for the meeting: has it become a habit? Could it be held less often? The most diplomatic way to reduce the size is to call no more meetings of this name or type and to restart with a smaller one of a new name, at a different regular time.

Reason

Ask yourself what the one key objective of the meeting is. This may involve standing back from the detail and questioning the overall direction and style of the meeting. You should also consider your personal reasons for holding the meeting: what do *you* want to get from it? For example, this could be to develop individuals, to change the group's perception of a subject or to get one particular action agreed.

Thinking carefully about the order of topics on the agenda can be worthwhile. Start with some easy items before tackling the controversial ones.

Environment

Make sure the room is the right temperature and will be free from interruptions. Arrange for visual aids like flipcharts, whiteboards and pens if possible.

Prompt start

Ensure a prompt start by assertiveness to latecomers – stop in midsentence as they come in, pause and then ask them why they are late for the meeting. Ask them if the other job could have been postponed or planned in for another time. Ask them if they could try to prevent it happening again. This awkward moment, though short and polite, will put the message across to everyone that prompt attendance is important to you. You cannot be seen to do nothing if someone arrives late, or it will become a habit for others too. If necessary, have a more serious talk to frequent latecomers privately later.

A prompt start is also more likely if you schedule the meeting for an unusual time like 10.15.

Urgency

The first two minutes set the tone of a meeting, so you should be conscious of this and make the effort to start crisply.

Start by summarizing the objective of the meeting. If possible, describe the successful outcome: 'By the end of this meeting we will have decided .../ come up with ideas for .../ all agreed a plan for ...'

Ideally the agenda has been sent in advance – check that everyone has one. The agenda should be a brief list of the points to be covered and the expected finish-time of the meeting. If necessary, give out more copies. Suggest and agree the approximate time that each item is likely to receive.

Control

For each topic, summarize the main arguments before opening it up for debate. Finish each item by summarizing again, agreeing any actions and making a note of who has agreed to do what and by when.

Regularly refer to the time spent so far and the number of items still to cover – is the meeting on schedule?

Use visual aids wherever possible. These give a focus to discussions, allow people who lose concentration to get back into the discussion, and also allow you to maintain control. Visual aids would ideally be flipcharts or whiteboards, but could also be diagrams or charts, of which copies are circulated (these do not generate quite the same team brainstorming feeling).

Control chatty or detail-orientated people by making sure they provide summaries, either in table form or preferably as visual graphs, having prepared these before the meeting.

End

Finish by agreeing the date of the next meeting, and thanking everyone for their time and the progress made. Ask them if it was a useful meeting.

Try to keep all meetings to an hour or less. Two hours is the absolute maximum permissible under any circumstances. Mental stamina declines rapidly after an hour, and your meetings should have a reputation for being dynamic not dreary! If there is more to discuss than can be fitted in, or new subjects come up unexpectedly, you can keep the extra subjects for another meeting.

IF YOU ARE NOT CHAIRING THE MEETING

Most meetings are chaired by someone else, and some of these can be extremely frustrating, but there are some tactics you could use.

Avoid going

Delegate attending the meeting to one of your team. Explain to the chairman before the meeting that you would like a member of your team to attend the meeting for experience and motivation.

Lobby the chairman before the meeting instead of going. Perhaps there is only one key point you want to communicate to them, or one action you want them to agree to. One-to-one lobbying can be much more time-efficient and can also get better results.

Ensure that the agenda is clear

Ask for an agenda in advance, 'so that you can prepare'. If necessary, ask to attend only for certain agenda items. If at the start of the meeting there is still no agenda, ask for the objectives of the meeting before starting.

Establish a finish-time

This is a reasonable request, as you need to plan your day. Explain at the start that you need to leave at the planned finish-time, or shortly after it. This clears the way for your leaving at that time, if you wish, without appearing rude. Of course, if the meeting has become interesting or useful you can always stay on.

Keep the meeting on track

The chairman should be doing this, but if they are not then anyone can help the chairman by doing it. Point out returns to previously agreed items: 'I thought we'd already agreed this one?' Point out red herrings: 'I'm sorry but I don't understand how this fits in with . . .' Point out excessive detail: 'Maybe this could be dealt with outside the meeting?'

Modify the structure of the meeting

Discuss the effectiveness of the meeting with the chairman afterwards – diplomatically! They may welcome a constructive discussion, having been uneasy about the meeting themselves. You could ask them whether they think the meeting could somehow cover the ground in a faster or more efficient way – perhaps by dividing it into two smaller meetings, or having it less often, or inviting fewer people, or producing a different type of agenda, minutes or actions list.

TYPES OF PEOPLE AND HOW TO GET THE BEST OUT OF THEM AT MEETINGS

Meetings are all about people, and each person is different – the fact that everyone needs a different management style is what makes management interesting. Any model of people and how to handle them is bound to be an approximation, but the following model is one that many managers have found useful. Although everyone is in reality somewhere on a sliding scale, we will class people as either introvert or extrovert, and either fact-based or feelings-based. The extroverts will be quicker to decide and more outspoken. The introverts will prefer to take their time in situations and will tend to be quieter. The fact-based thinkers will be at home with numbers, machines and practicalities, and their decisions will tend to be logical; while the feelings-based people will prefer to deal with people and their decisions will be more emotional.

This gives four combinations, as shown below – which box would you put yourself in, and where would you put your close friends, colleagues and partner?

	Introvert	*Extrovert*
Facts		
Feelings		

The types who occupy each of the four boxes can be described briefly as follows:

	Introvert	*Extrovert*
Facts	Analytical This person likes to know all the detail before making a decision. Accuracy is important to them.	Controller This person likes to know the key points and then get on with making the decision and taking action. Results are important to them.
Feelings	Supporter This person likes to get to know the people involved before making decisions. Good relationships are important to them.	Enthusiast This person likes the excitement of new possibilities and makes quick, confident decisions based on the overall feel of the situation.

The analytical tends to find the enthusiast much too disorganized and emotional, while the enthusiast finds the analytical dry and fussy. On the other diagonal, the supporter finds the controller hard and ruthless, while the controller finds the supporter too slow and too soft. But it takes all types to make a good team, and all four have their strengths.

The analytical

This is the person to give the detail work to. They will be thorough, fair, organized, and will be the least likely to make mistakes. When presenting information they may need some help in making it brief, clear and interesting. They are good at spotting potential technical problems in plans. They will also be good at taking detailed minutes, if you need these. However, brief notes of actions will often be enough, and these are the strength of the controller.

The controller

This is the person to whom you can delegate tasks if they are tough or need pushing through in a short time. They can be given the job of heading a sub-team to sort out a particular problem that comes up. They are liable to get impatient in meetings, but this can be used to your advantage if you ask them how long a job is likely to take or whether they feel that the obstacles can be overcome. They may be worth talking to before the meeting to make sure they are on your side.

The supporter

The strength of supporters is their ability to think through the people-implications of plans – this may sometimes be seen as negative or cautious but can be very valuable in avoiding problems later. Most plans go wrong because of people! They may need to be encouraged to speak up and give their opinion. They can appear to slow meetings down, which will frustrate controllers and enthusiasts. Their views may not be logically supported with facts, but will be well judged and carefully considered.

The enthusiast

These are the best motivators in the group, and are likely to be creative and optimistic. They are likely to agree to take on actions, but will need to be monitored and reminded later. They are the most likely to commit themselves to aiming at ambitious goals. They are prone to wasting time at meetings by going off track.

As you can see, without one of the above your group will be without analysis, drive, feel or enthusiasm, so they all have their place. In fact, while the diagonally opposing types may have difficulty understanding each other they can make excellent complimentary partnerships. Partnerships across the upper and lower horizontals may lack feeling or rigour, respectively, while partnerships vertically on the left and on the right may lack drive or be too rushed, respectively.

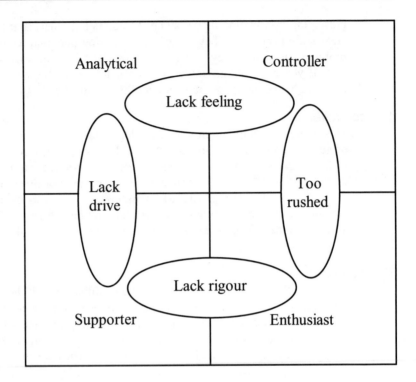

When planning a team you would ideally select at least one of each type, and in a meeting where not all types are represented you should modify your own input to fill the gap.

In terms of personal time management, the four types have the following areas of potential weakness:

	Introvert	*Extrovert*
Facts	Analytical Too much of a perfectionist Need to think bigger (see chapter 2) Procrastination due to waiting to have perfect information	Controller Imbalance between work and home, and between achievement and quality of life Need to learn to relax and enjoy the present
Feelings	Supporter Not good at saying no Need to focus on their own objectives rather than letting/helping others achieve theirs Procrastination due to fear of problems with people	Enthusiast Disorganized Lack of planning Procrastination of unpleasant tasks due to lack of self-discipline; temptation to do easier tasks instead

This model of personality types is also useful in many other areas of management – you may like to think about how you would motivate each of the four types or negotiate with them.

In chapter 9 we will be looking at personality drivers as a cause of stress. You may notice a link between controllers and the 'hurry up' and 'be strong' drivers, analyticals and the 'be perfect' driver, supporters and 'please others'. The main source of stress for the enthusiast is likely to be lack of self-discipline leading to taking on too much while neglecting their fitness, diet and sleep.

ACTION PLANS

Meetings can be an excellent management tool if they are used correctly.

- What are you going to do differently at the meetings that you chair?

- Are there any meetings that you could abolish or make less frequent?

- Are there any subjects or teams which would benefit from a meeting?

- Which meetings that you attend are too slow or not constructive? What actions are you going to take to do something about these?

- Which of the four personality types is missing from the meetings that you chair or attend?

- Who at your meetings could have the strengths of their personality type better used, and how?

8 Delegation: the key to multiplying your time

This chapter is structured into the following sections:
- why delegate?
- why we avoid delegating
- the signs of being a poor delegator
- are your team members ready?
- helping them to move towards freedom
- the techniques
- the traps
- watch out for the monkey
- delegating to difficult people
- action plans.

WHY DELEGATE?

The advantages of delegation are immense. Here are some.
- achieve ten or twenty times as much
- find better quality solutions by using the skills of your team
- increase the motivation of your team by involvement and ownership
- develop an even more capable team
- survival as a manager – you simply *cannot* do everything yourself.

Correct delegation will *not* make your job redundant, because you will still be the initiator and controller, the leader with vision who is generating the results. Only abdication will make your job redundant, and that is *not* the same as delegation, as we shall see.

WHY WE AVOID DELEGATING

Here is a list of the main reasons for not delegating, either conscious or subconscious. How many of them do you find yourself sometimes slipping into?

131

Reason for not delegating tasks	1 Disagree: not an issue for me	2 Sometimes agree: occasional reason	3 Major reason for not delegating	4 Agree totally: always true for me
I'm better than them at the task, and we want the best possible job done				
I enjoy doing an easy and quick task every now and then (it's much easier than my own job!)				
I am worried that they'll make a mess of it, and it's too important to take that risk				
If they make a mess of it I'll get the blame				
If they do well they'll get the glory (and it was *my* idea!)				
My boss likes to see me getting stuck in				
I need to show my people that I know what I'm talking about				
If I delegate it I won't know the details of the job and I need to know these for my boss/customer				
By the time I've explained it it's quicker if I just get on and do it myself				
If I do it myself I get it done exactly right and exactly how I wanted it done				

Reason for not delegating tasks	1	2	3	4
I feel uncomfortable about asking them to do tasks for me				
If they do a job for me I'll then owe them favours				
They're too busy/overworked already				

If you ticked columns 3 or 4 I would like to present the counter-arguments, as follows:

'I'm better than them at the job, and we want the best possible job done.' This may only be your opinion, but even if it *is* true you can't do *every* job yourself. If you try to do everything you will end up swamped and doing some jobs badly. By delegating this job you will have the time to do another more important job properly. The person who is doing this job for you will be able to learn, until one day they can do it as well as you can.

'I enjoy doing an easy and quick job every now and then (it's much easier than my own job!).' You are entitled to some fun as long as you recognize it is as such. There is a cost to having this fun, which is that a more important job is not being done, and you are also demotivating the person who *should* be doing this job.

'I am worried that they'll make a mess of it, and it's too important to take that risk.' Later in this chapter we will look at monitoring and the concept of grip. You can delegate a task and still maintain control by monitoring progress. If you have worries about the ability of the person you can use very frequent monitoring or employ a coaching style of shared decision-making.

'If they make a mess of it I'll get the blame.' Yes, and so you should! If it goes wrong, *you* must have either selected the wrong person or not monitored progress and supported them correctly. But this fear will be unfounded if you delegate properly and maintain sufficient grip – the job cannot go wrong in a serious way, because when it starts to drift off course you can step in and correct it.

'If they do well they'll get the glory (and it was *my* idea!).' You will get your share of recognition if you defined, delegated, monitored and reported on the progress of the task to your boss. If you make sure that the individuals who did the work get the credit for it, some of this will rub off on you too. A rising tide raises all ships, and only a weak (abdicating) manager is not credited with the success of their team. But even if you receive no recognition for the results of your team you should still be satisfied, because you have made progress towards your objectives – everything you delegate should be linked to your objectives.

'My boss likes to see me getting stuck in.' As described in detail in chapter 6, your relationship with your boss should be above this, and it is your responsibility to handle it. You can explain to your boss that you are planning to delegate a certain task to a certain person in order to develop them and free yourself up to do more important work, and check that your boss agrees.

'I need to show my people that I know what I'm talking about.' Your team need to understand that you are the type of boss who trusts them to do what they do best, and that you will stand back and plan for their long-term wellbeing rather than get dragged into every little job. It's not that you don't care – you *do* – but you know that the best way to get results is to let them do the job without interference. You will need to be open with your team in explaining this management philosophy, which is good for them as well as for you and the organization.

'If I delegate it I won't know the details of the job, and I need to know these for my boss or customer.' Find out what level of reporting they require and which areas they will want to know about. Check up on progress of key points before the meeting. If necessary bring the person to whom you have delegated the work to the meeting too. Make sure that the progress of the project is being judged on measurable outcomes rather than your boss's or the customer's opinions of the methods being used.

'By the time I've explained it it's quicker if I just get on and do it myself.' This is true, but only once. You will reap the long-term benefits if you make the effort to develop your people.

'If I do it myself I get it done exactly right and exactly how I wanted it done.' Letting go is one of the difficult aspects of delegation, especially if you have a strong 'be perfect' driver (see chapter 9). Part of 'exactly right' will be only your opinion of what the customer wants, the rest will be specifiable on paper and can be given as instructions to whoever you give the job to. But before you specify the job too tightly, consider asking them how *they* would do it – perhaps they have ideas that are surprisingly good?

'I feel uncomfortable about asking them to do tasks for me.' Analyse your reason for feeling uncomfortable. If you feel that the person is too busy, see below. If you feel that the task is an unpleasant one, decide whether they are the best person for the job and tell them why you have chosen them. 'Best' could mean the person who will learn most from it, not necessarily the one who can do it most easily. You may be able to find someone who will enjoy the particular task that you find unpleasant. You may need to share it out equally among everyone. You should certainly not delegate all the unpleasant work and keep the fun parts for yourself. But conversely, you should not let the results of the organization be compromised by an unwillingness to face up to giving out unpopular work. Remember, if you do this job, which really should be delegated, you are then unable to do a more important one.

'If they do a job for me I'll owe them favours.' Maybe you feel that your position will be weaker when they ask for a pay rise or time off, or if they try to avoid another job in the future. But this feeling is totally in your own head. Your decisions on concessions should be made on the total of the person's work, rather than on single incidents like whether you delegated work to them.

'They're too busy/overworked already.' There are a number of points to consider before conceding this:

- Do you work longer hours than them? If so, this is *not* what you are paid for. You are paid to take a longer-term view and to make bigger decisions. You are paid for results, not for time. Maybe you have not got the delegation balance right?
- How do you know they are fully loaded? They will certainly be busy when you are around!
- If their workload was reduced by 10 per cent, would they sit around for an hour a day? Probably not. The other work would expand to fill the time, by a combination of better quality and slower pace. So, even though everyone would be busy all of the time on the remaining 90 per cent, we know that it would be possible to squeeze in another 10 per cent and get back to where you are now. So how do you know that there isn't room for another 10 per cent at

the moment? If you feel you have pushed them to the maximum, how do you know for sure?

■ Could they work more effectively? Are they working to every single principle in this book? Can you help them to work more effectively? Giving them more work could push them to work more effectively.

■ If they did some jobs less well, but fitted others in, would there be a net gain?

■ If they needed an extra hour per day to gather diamonds in the car park but could not work longer hours, would they find a way to fit this in? I think so!

THE SIGNS OF BEING A POOR DELEGATOR

Suppose you are not delegating as much as you could or should do. How would you know? Poor delegation normally shows up only in the long term, when, despite a lot of hard work, results are poorer than expected. However, there are some short-term symptoms that are worth watching out for.

Exercise:
Which of the following apply to you?

❑ You feel busy, to the point of only just keeping up.

❑ Your desk is untidy, to the point where some important papers are covered by others.

❑ You are the 'key person', the one 'in the know', essential at every crisis meeting etc.

❑ You know every detail of what's going on in your area.

❑ There are frequent interruptions by subordinates with questions about the job, or requests for advice or decisions.

> ❑ They can't do it themselves: you have to tell them what to do and how to do it.
>
> ❑ You regularly work longer hours than your team.
>
> ❑ You find that other people cannot attain the high standards that you would ideally like and which you achieve if you do the job yourself.
>
> If you felt that two or more of the above described you, then you should actively consider whether you could delegate more. If you have reasons why you cannot delegate more, then you may be using one of the excuses mentioned earlier. If you are, evaluate it hard and think 'Is it really a valid reason?'

Assuming you are going to delegate more, the first step is to look at the people available to do the work for you.

ARE YOUR TEAM MEMBERS READY?

You probably have some members of your team to whom you can delegate all sorts of responsible work, and some others who you believe can handle very little. Imagine if they could all do everything that you currently have on your desk! You would be free to plan ahead, take on more interesting or demanding projects, or reduce your working hours. You would be free to choose how to spend your time. This must be the ultimate objective of any manager who values their time.

There are two reasons why some of your subordinates cannot handle work which you would like to delegate to them: lack of *competence* and lack of *motivation*. Either they are not yet able to do it on their own or they are not committed enough to be trusted with the work. Once you are clear which of these two areas needs development you are one step nearer to the goal of maximum delegation. This process benefits all concerned, because your team members themselves would *also* like to be competent and motivated. Some of the reasons why people might be in each category are shown in the diagram below.

	Not competent	*Competent*
Motivated	New starter Recently promoted At limit of current ability	Experienced
Not motivated	Finding job harder than expected Bad treatment by previous manager In wrong position Job is incorrectly designed Lack of training	Been in job a long time Passed over for promotion Bad treatment by previous manager Insecure in job

Before we look at how to manage each of the types, write the names of your team in the boxes. Also, which box are *you* in?

There is an ideal management style for each of the four types, as shown below:

	Not competent	*Competent*
Motivated	*Tell* Tell them what to do Because they are motivated they will do it Give clear instructions, followed by praise Plan to move them across to the next box gradually	*Delegate* Delegate large tasks Monitor loosely Thank and reward Make sure they know they are in this box and that you appreciate it
Not motivated	*Coach* Explain that you will be coaching them in order that they can learn Teach them what you do in your job: how and why. Ask them for their ideas on problems and give praise when they are right Give them tasks, but check their planned actions before they take them	*Involve* Involve them in your decisions Value their knowledge and make sure they know you do Thank them for their help Make sure they get the credit for their ideas and any joint ideas, not you Appoint them as a deputy on a major task of yours

The key difference between coaching and involvement is that with coaching *you* are providing most of the information and making the decisions, but with involvement *they* are providing most of the information while *you* still make the decisions. In practice there will be a sliding scale between these two boxes, as they gradually provide more of the information, but in all cases you control the decisions. Only with delegation do *they* make the decisions.

It is possible to move from any of the boxes gradually into the top right box, as shown in the next section.

HELPING INDIVIDUALS MOVE UP TO FREEDOM

The following diagram shows how your team members can move up from 'wait until told', which could be due to lack of knowledge or lack of motivation, to 'free to act', which requires both competence and motivation. Someone can therefore move into the top right box of the previous diagram from any of the other three boxes, by moving up this ladder.

THE FREEDOM LADDER

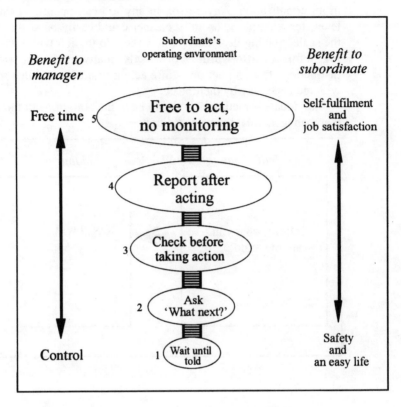

Where do you want to be? Where do you want the members of your team to be?

For the manager, the advantage of keeping people at the bottom of the scale is control, but this is counteracted, and outweighed, by the benefit of *more time* and a motivated team, which is achieved by helping the subordinates reach self-fulfilment at the top. Moving your team members up the ladder allows you to escape from box 2 (urgent but unimportant) activities like supervision, checking, instructing and problem solving, and to spend more time in box 3 (longer-term important activities like planning ahead and improving underlying systems).

For the individual, the perceived loss of safety and 'an easy life' is rewarded by self-fulfilment and job satisfaction.

Note: this scale should not be connected in any way with status in an organization. Any person in any job can operate at this top level; for example, a lavatory cleaner could easily be at the top of the scale, making decisions on how they do the job without reporting before or afterwards. Conversely, many managers wait for instructions from higher up before acting or are treated in a 'check with me first' way by their boss.

Individuals sometimes choose to be at the bottom, with the result that managers treat them accordingly.

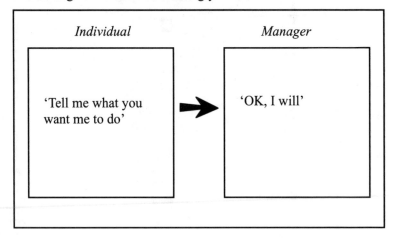

A circle follows, and there is no way this circle can be broken by the *individual*; it is up to the *manager* to give them the freedom to move up, with the accompanying risk. If an individual is used to being up at level 4 or 5 and is then treated inappropriately, for example criticized unfairly for a wrong decision, they can easily retreat to a lower level and take the attitude 'OK then, you tell me what you want me to do next time'. So it is easy for an individual to move down, and more difficult for them to move up. It is up to the manager to help (or drag) the individual up the ladder. Here are some examples of the steps that the manager can take to move someone up the ladder.

Level 1 to level 2

Giving them responsibility for their work loading:

- take an interest in their progress
- explain the importance of what they are doing and how it fits into the bigger picture
- ask them what level of quality they feel they can achieve
- involve them in some of the planning
- ask them to estimate completion times.

Level 2 to level 3

Encouraging them to provide suggestions and become involved in decisions:

- show that you value their opinions
- explain that you would like them to become more involved in the decisions that are made
- ask for suggestions and solutions rather than problems
- make sure they are clear on their level of authority, and in which areas they must check before taking action.

Level 3 to level 4

Allowing them the first step of autonomy, initially on low-risk tasks, then on increasingly large ones:

- praise their recent performance
- explain that in this particular area there is no need for them to check with you first
- ask them to keep you informed by letting you know when they take actions (after they have taken them).

Level 4 to level 5

The reporting rate can gradually be reduced from 'straight after every time' to a weekly summary of events, then monthly:

■ 'There's no need to tell me each time, just go ahead and do what you think is right and we'll have a meeting once a week/month to discuss progress. OK?'

Note: Individuals can be at different levels for different aspects of their job. For example, a Production Manager might

■ be free to talk to suppliers whenever he/she pleases (level 5)
■ be able to take disciplinary action when necessary but have to report it afterwards (level 4)
■ need to obtain authorization before recruiting new personnel (level 3)
■ make suggestions as to improvements in sales or finance (level 2)
■ wait to hear from the top concerning the long-term vision for the organization (level 1).

The ability to stand back and think about longer-term trends and underlying structures is known as 'helicopter view'. One aspect of taking this view is to think about which levels your people are currently on and to consider whether they can be moved up at all in order to give *them* more motivation and *yourself* more time.

THE DELEGATION PROCESS

For individuals to whom you can delegate, it is important to get the process right. Here are the six stages to successful delegation.

Select the right tasks

Delegate as many as possible, including the ones *you* like! Question every task that you do with 'Could I delegate it?' If not, ask yourself 'Who would do it if I were away for three months?' and then consider giving it to them.

Select the right person

Select someone who will find the task a challenge, and who will therefore gain a sense of achievement from completing it.

Brief them correctly

Write the finished requirements down for them. Explain the value, how the job fits in with the overall picture. Don't specify the method; leave that to the person to decide. Make clear the limits of authority that they are being given. Gain commitment:

- do they understand what is required?
- do they feel they can do it?
- are they going to do it?
- how long do they think it will take?

Agree a timescale for the whole job, and agree the frequency of monitoring progress.

Monitor progress

If you have to keep asking 'How is it getting on?' you will feel like a pest, you will tend to avoid asking and you may end up losing grip. 'Grip' is the level of awareness you maintain over the progress of a task that you have delegated; it is not sinister or restricting, but is merely the degree of monitoring and support you provide in order to make sure that the job is completed successfully with no sudden or expensive surprises.

An excellent way to maintain grip is to have a regular one-to-one progress-review session. If necessary this could be at a fixed time every day, just for five minutes, or alternatively at each meeting you could set the time for the next one ('How long do you think it will take before you finish the next step? OK, we'll meet just after then, on Wednesday the 21st at 9 a.m., OK?').

A less obtrusive way to maintain grip is to ask for a graph to be kept on the wall and updated every day, so that you can walk past and check it whenever you need to. You only need to disturb them to congratulate them on progress or to investigate problems.

A weekly meeting is an essential part of managing any team, and it also has the advantage that you can maintain grip by asking each person to report briefly to the group on their progress since the last meeting.

A monthly report is also an excellent way to monitor progress. Ask them to keep it very brief, perhaps just one page of typed information.

When monitoring, resist getting drawn in or interfering, unless they ask for help or there is a serious risk of an expensive problem which cannot be fixed afterwards.

Support when necessary

Make sure they know that you are genuinely available for support.

Always be positive about problems – they can always be solved, and they are an opportunity to learn and improve. Thank them for letting you know about problems. If you are negative or aggressive about problems or mistakes, then your team will be reluctant to tell you about them. If you detect a problem that they have not told you about, ask probing questions about progress until they admit the problem, then solve it together positively. Ask for them to tell you about it next time.

Review and praise

Establish a habit of reviewing tasks afterwards: what went well, what went badly, how can we learn and do better next time. This is not about judging the person, but about taking an objective view of the task and the person's skills and needs for future development.

Always find something to praise in the work they have done; this is the key to improving their motivation. It also improves their skills by reinforcing the positive actions and neglecting to reinforce the errors.

THE DELEGATION TRAPS

Here are the main traps to watch out for in the above process.

Possession

This is to fail to delegate a job because you can't let it go. You may rationalize with 'It's too important' or 'I need to be seen to be doing this one', but the reality of possession is probably that you enjoy it, or that you enjoy the glory of the results, or that you need the security of the occasional easy job. But remember that possession holds you back from achieving your objectives because it makes you work on the tasks that are less important.

Now ask yourself 'Do I hang on to jobs?'

❏   Never   ❏   Sometimes   ❏   Often

Viewpoint

It is an error to plan delegation from your point of view rather than theirs. The result will be that you tend to delegate the jobs that *you* don't want to do, rather than the jobs that *they* will benefit from. Can you see this job from their point of view? Will they be motivated to do it? How will they do it? Which aspects will they find difficult, and what problems will they have?

Now ask yourself 'Do I forget their point of view?'

❏   Never   ❏   Sometimes   ❏   Often

Guilt

Reluctance to give out jobs that may be difficult or unpleasant will force you to do them yourself and you then won't have enough time for more important matters.

Now ask yourself 'Does guilt prevent me delegating?'

❏   Never   ❏   Sometimes   ❏   Often

Rush

It is a mistake is to spend too little time at the beginning of the delegation process. Have they got clear directions? Have you checked that they have understood the job, that they feel they can do it and that they are going to do it?

Now ask yourself 'Do I do fail to brief carefully enough?'

❏   Never   ❏   Sometimes   ❏   Often

Detail

It is a mistake to tell them everything about how you want the job done. How do you know that they can't do it even better in a different way? They will be demotivated if they feel that you don't trust them to plan it and make decisions for themselves. So even if you know exactly how the job should be done you must keep quiet and let them decide this for themselves. Tell them what you want the *result* to be like, not *how* to do it. This is the difference between delegating and telling.

Now ask yourself 'Do I tell them too much?'

❏   Never   ❏   Sometimes   ❏   Often

Perhaps you are absolutely certain you know how the job needs to be done. Then why are you wasting an experienced and motivated person on this job? You may as well give it to a new starter, with full instructions.

Trust

Belief in others is necessary in order to encourage and motivate them, but there may come a point where you delegate important tasks to people who either are not up to it in terms of competence or cannot be trusted with a task at this level.

Now ask yourself 'Do I delegate jobs that I should have kept and done myself?'

❏   Never   ❏   Sometimes   ❏   Often

This only becomes a major problem if it is combined with a lack of grip.

Grip

Insufficient grip means that you don't know enough about what they are doing and you just hope that it works out OK (it won't!).

Now ask yourself 'Do I let my grip become weak?'

❏   Never   ❏   Sometimes   ❏   Often

Too much grip means that you monitor too closely and interfere whenever you feel that the job is not going quite right. Sometimes the job will not be done as well as you would have done it. Sometimes it will be done differently from the way you would have done it. You will have to live with this (how is your 'be perfect' driver? – see next chapter); but remember that if ten jobs are done by others at only remaining 30 per cent efficiency, this still gives you a leverage factor of seven times, particularly as most of the 70 per cent ('they didn't do it as well as I would have') is probably only in your perception!

Now ask yourself 'Do I grip too tightly?'

❏   Never   ❏   Sometimes   ❏   Often

Worry

Worry about whether delegated tasks will be ready on time and/or up to the required level of quality arises mainly from lack of grip. If you monitor progress correctly, worry will not be a part of the delegation process.

Now ask yourself 'Do I end up worrying about jobs I have delegated?'

❏   Never   ❏   Sometimes   ❏   Often

Blame

If the job goes wrong, never blame the person you delegated it to. It is *your* fault. Either you chose the wrong person, or you failed to explain the task clearly enough, or you did not provide sufficient resources, or you did not monitor closely enough, or you did not provide the support and guidance when needed. If something could have been done and wasn't done, then *you* should have done it. *You* are to blame. If you blame the person you delegated to, they will tend to hide problems from you next time instead of coming to you for support. They will also not be keen to work for you again, and if they do they will slide down into 'Tell me what to do next'.

Now ask yourself 'Do I blame people for their problems or their failures?'

❏   Never   ❏   Sometimes   ❏   Often

THE MONKEY

Some subordinates will resist having work delegated to them even if you do it correctly. They are capable of doing the work but they intend to avoid doing it. This is where firmness and a certain amount of games-playing is needed, as follows . . .

When someone comes to you with a problem, you can picture it as an invisible monkey on their back. If you say 'OK, leave it with me' or 'I'll find out and let you know', you have just added another monkey to the hoard already on your back. These will make your progress towards your objectives slower and your stress level higher. If it's a genuine request for help, then you may need to take it. But it is very important that you don't let anyone give you a monkey unless you really want to have it.

Monkey-givers could be colleagues or subordinates. (Of your subordinates, the competent but not motivated person is the one to watch.) Your boss is the only person who is allowed to give you monkeys, and even then you may decide to try to resist them. (For managing your boss, saying no and negotiating one monkey for another, see chapter 6.) Below are the first steps you should take in order to make sure that they keep the monkey.

When they ask to discuss a complicated problem (with the intention of you solving it for them) ask for a summary of the problem, written on one sheet of A4. Ask when they can do it by, and arrange a meeting for then. They go out of your office with the monkey still firmly on their back.

When you get a summary of a problem, either in writing or verbally, ask them to make a list of suggested solutions. Ask when they can do it by, and arrange a meeting for then. They go out of your office with the monkey still firmly on their back.

When they ask for you, with your power as the manager who controls key resources, to implement a solution give *them* the authority to implement it, if necessary by giving them a written note or making a phone call there and then, while they wait. Once this is done, ask when they can do it by, and arrange a meeting for then. They go out of your office with the monkey still firmly on their back.

If there are forms to be filled in (e.g. application for capital expenditure) give them the form and ask them to fill it in and bring it back for you to sign when it's done. Ask when they can do it by, and arrange a meeting for then. They go out of your office with the monkey still firmly on their back.

Can you see a pattern emerging? Notice how you are leaving the next action with them, whilst maintaining grip by setting the next date for feedback. You know what is happening at all times, and you make sure they are under pressure to do what they have said they will do. If they object to the process at any point, saying you are the boss and it's your job to solve problems and make decisions, explain that you *are* the boss and in your opinion it is *their* job. You do not have time to do their job for them, and *you* decide which tasks it is more efficient for them to do.

Think of a subordinate who gives you monkeys, and try these techniques out. Think 'monkey' when you next see him or her. You will enjoy the process, and it will bring you good results.

DELEGATING TO DIFFICULT PEOPLE

Rather than monkey-givers who are simply avoiding taking on work, there are many other types who are difficult to delegate to, often due to aspects of their personality or behaviour of which they are unaware. Here are the main ones, with possible strategies. Do you know any of these?

The complainer

They complain about being given the job, or about the obstacles to achieving it that the organization puts in their path. This person is often competent but not motivated, so the involving style should be your first tactic. Remember that trusting them with delegation is very risky. If they are negative about even the smallest job you give them, ask for a list (written) of all of the problems. Then ask them for suggested cost-effective solutions to their list. Force them to be constructive. Explain that you don't want to hear complaints without suggestions. Depending on the suggestions, you can then either ask if they think the list is realistic (what will it cost, how long will it take, who will do it, etc.), implement it yourself or, better still, give *them* the job of implementing it. Make them realize that they are responsible for their own lives, both in terms of what happens to them and whether they enjoy or dislike the process.

If complaints of a more general nature persist, ask what they want; what would they put in the place of the present situation? If necessary, ask if they like working here, all things considered. If the answer is no, you can help them find another job.

The optimistic promiser

Dangerous! You may have to be caught out once or twice before you realize that you are dealing with one of these. But once you do, you can ask them for a plan for each job they are doing, written down, with steps to be taken, milestones (perhaps a Gantt chart) and a cumulative expenditure graph. It takes you none of your time to have this done, and as well as giving you control it will also help them to monitor progress. Then ask them to report regularly on progress and to keep the graph updated on their wall so you can look at it whenever you need to. Explain that you don't want a repeat of the previous problem, and that doing this will be good for both of you and for the organization.

The pessimist

A useful team member, since they will plan ahead and help you avoid potential problems. Ask for a list of potential problems whenever you have a plan, and then ask them for ideas on how the problem could be averted. If you are busy, you could ask them to go away and write these lists, bringing them back the next day for you to look at.

The skunk

This person's game is to resist change in their area of expertise by making life difficult for you if you interfere – 'Leave me alone and I won't give you any trouble' – perhaps bringing every problem to you when they know that you don't have the detailed knowledge to make correct decisions. The answer is to have a 'little chat' and explain that their area is going to have to change, whether they like it or not. Explain why. Explain that their position is safe, and that you respect their knowledge and intend to keep them for it. Then ask them to set goals for themselves: what improvements do they feel they can achieve? People tend to set quite demanding targets for themselves if they do not feel under threat, but if they do come up with cautious goals you can then explain that these are not enough. Then monitor progress by asking them to report to you, probably once a week, on what has happened, potential problems and progress towards objectives. Make sure that they understand that the weekly meeting must be attended at all costs and that failure to report all significant events will not be appreciated.

The vague drifter

These are the people who just don't seem to get motivated, whatever you do. They do the basic job in a minimum way, and are only just doing enough to justify their employment. Ask them to set their own objectives, correcting these upwards if necessary. Find ways to measure their achievements numerically, and put these on a graph on the wall. Try to find out what does excite them, and use this in the design of their job. As a last resort, consider moving them to a different job in the hope that they will come to life there.

The yes man

Ask yourself whether you are frightening them, either accidentally or deliberately, by your management style? Consider going to see them rather than summoning them to your office when you need to talk to them. Instead of asking for their opinion of *your* plan, ask for *their* plan. What do they think should be done in this situation? If you need to ask them to review your plan, ask them for their *honest* opinion. Ask them what they think might go wrong. Ask them to help you spot any snags in your plan. Make it easy for them to disagree.

The 'yes but' excuse-giver

These people tend to ask you for help, but every suggestion you make is met with 'I've tried that' or 'That won't work because . . .' Before suggesting solutions, your first step is to ask what they have already tried and to decide whether they are competent or not. If you believe that they are, use the *involving* style in an assertive way by saying 'I'm not going to make suggestions; you're the one with the experience, you solve it. I want you to come back tomorrow with a plan for me to approve (or a choice of plans)'. If you feel that they are not competent, then use a *coaching* style: explain what you plan to do and why. Ask if they have any better ideas, and, if not, go ahead and implement your plan.

The headless chicken

This person always seems incredibly busy – too busy to help you in fact – and they try to make you feel guilty when you ask them for one more job. Help them to improve by first of all confirming with them that they do not have enough time to get everything done properly. Explain that they appear to have a time-management problem, and that it needs to be solved since it is affecting their performance (they may not have become aware of it before). Explain that you will help them. Ask to see their work plan: make sure they have a diary and a daily jobs-to-do list. Ask to see these regularly until they have learned to organize themselves.

The checker

This person checks everything with you first, to cover themselves if anything goes wrong. Explain to them that you don't have time to do their job as well as your own. Explain that you have faith in them to do the job correctly (providing that you do). Define carefully what they can do on their own and what they need to check with you first, and write this down. Consider getting them to write a short note to you after each major action they take, to keep you informed. If you have reason to doubt their capability, then checking what they do is a good idea but is best controlled by a daily or weekly coaching meeting where you discuss their plans and help them discover the best solutions.

The detail person

This person wants everything defined in advance and wants to talk about everything at length. Explain that you only have a certain amount of time for each person who works for you, on average (for example, ten people each taking an hour a day would mean you could do nothing else). Set them clear but brief objectives and explain that it is up to them how they achieve them. Whenever they come to ask questions explain that you are pushed for time and send them away with the task of writing a quarter-page summary of the problem or suggesting solutions on paper, one page of A4 maximum. You can explain that this is the way that you like to work.

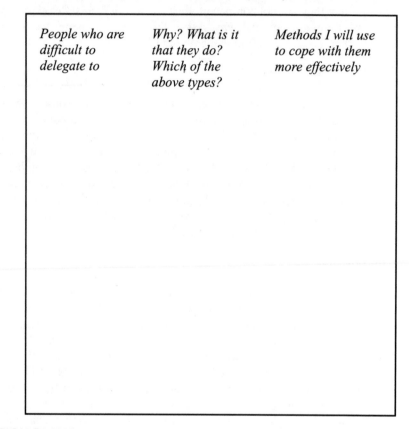

People who are difficult to delegate to	*Why? What is it that they do? Which of the above types?*	*Methods I will use to cope with them more effectively*

ACTION PLANS

In this chapter we have looked at the effects that you and other people can have on your ability to delegate successfully. It is a vitally important management skill, more of a science than many people realize, but not as difficult as it may appear when reading about it. The following action plan will help you identify your areas for improvement, and will repay a little time and thought.

■ My favourite reason for not delegating as much as I should:

Is it a sufficient reason for not delegating? ❑ No ❑ No!

■ One job I should delegate but which I tend to do myself *because I enjoy it*:

■ One job I should delegate but which I find hard to let go because it needs to be done with *very high quality*:

■ One job I should delegate but which would require *considerable time* to explain and to train the person for:

■ One job that *might go wrong* if I delegated it:

Would close monitoring allow successful delegation?
❑ Yes ❑ Yes!

■ Is there anyone who uses 'appearing busy' as a defence against being delegated more work?

■ One person I will use the coaching style with:

■ One person I will help to move up the freedom ladder, and how I will do it:

■ The method of monitoring that I will use:

Idea: if you have subordinates who are managers, give them this chapter to read and ask them to fill out the action plan. Ask them to estimate when they can have it done by, and set a meeting for then.

9 Stress: how high is yours and what can be done?

In this chapter we will examine stress from the time management point of view. The objective of the chapter is to discover the causes of undue stress in yourself, to help you decide where your optimum stress level is and to generate ideas and an action plan for how you will get your stress level right. This may not necessarily mean reducing your stress, since a certain level of stress can be good for you. There is a close link between excess stress and poor time management, and since time management is within your control you can also have a significant effect on your stress levels by using the right techniques. Poor time management is a *source* of stress, whilst good time management is important in *coping* with stress, so time management appears on both sides of the stress balance. The chapter is divided into the following seven sections:

- analysing your current situation: how do you feel about your current level of stress? What symptoms of stress do you exhibit, if any?
- sources of stress, controllable or not controllable, internally or externally generated
- discovering your personality driver, a possible cause of additional stress
- your ability to cope with stress: the balance between what's coming in and your ability to cope with it, and the link between the two
- how your stress level varies during the day
- thinking about your optimum level of stress: the effect of stress on your rate of achievement and your quality of life, and the trade-off between the two
- techniques for reducing your current stress level.

ANALYSING YOUR CURRENT SITUATION

Where would you put yourself on the following line at present?

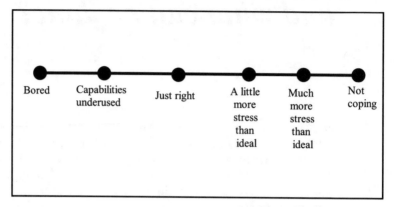

Is the stress that you currently have produced mainly by work or home?

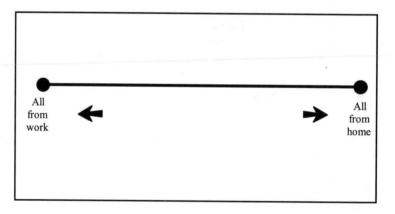

Exercise:
How many of the following symptoms of stress do you exhibit?

Symptoms at work
❑ long working hours during the week, not out of choice
❑ working on Saturdays 'to keep up with the job'
❑ bringing work home
❑ not taking all holidays entitled to
❑ cancelling booked holidays due to work crisis
❑ desk covered in paperwork – important items hidden by others
❑ feeling that you can't rely on or trust your team to get the job done without you

Behavioural signs
❑ thinking about work while going to sleep (perhaps keeping a pad by the bed and switching the light back on to make notes when thoughts come to you)
❑ drinking to relax
❑ driving: tendency to become angry or impatient with other drivers
❑ house untidy, some areas out of control

Physical signs
❑ reduced energy – putting off tackling problems
❑ more accident prone or clumsy than usual
❑ reduced sex drive due to work tiredness or work thoughts
❑ physically overweight or unfit
❑ general feeling of uneasiness in shoulders or stomach

Mental signs
❑ constant nagging feeling of too much to do and not enough time
❑ difficulty concentrating on one thing at a time
❑ occasional angry outburst – 'the last straw' – or tendency to snap
❑ unable to relax and enjoy peaceful situations
❑ reduced sense of humour in difficult situations

SOURCES OF STRESS

Surveys have shown the following to be the top ten life events for causing stress:

- death of spouse
- divorce
- prison sentence
- death of close family member
- personal injury or illness
- marriage
- redundancy or dismissal
- retirement
- pregnancy
- money problems.

These major events are mainly uncontrollable, and beyond the scope of this book. However, good time management may be able to help you reduce your stress level whilst coping with them. Fortunately, for most people their day to day stress comes from a collection of much smaller sources than the above, and many of these are linked to personal time management. What are *your* main causes of stress at present? These could be people, situations or activities. Try to fill in the box before looking at the suggestions given on the next page.

Exercise:
My main causes of stress are:

Here are some ideas for causes of stress, large and small, that you may not have remembered to add to your personal list:

- money
- relationships
- ageing
- health
- deadlines approaching
- lack of personal organization
- unclear direction in job or life generally
- driving, traffic
- using aggression as a method of getting your own way
- not being assertive enough, and regretting it later
- uncertainty at work: attitude of boss or future of company
- unhappy with type of work
- feeling of not fitting in with the organizational culture
- tiredness
- being late
- being stuck in meetings when other jobs are waiting to be done
- fear of failure
- being a naturally impatient person
- working atmosphere: noisy, cramped or otherwise unsuitable
- untidy/cluttered environment at home or at work
- nobody of a like mind to bounce ideas off
- nobody you can rely on
- lack of control
- loose ends/not having time to finish jobs properly.

From the two lists, identify some sources of stress that you would like to deal with, and complete the first half of the following table. In the rest of this chapter we will be looking at ways to help you complete the second column of the table.

Five causes of stress that I really need to deal with	*How could these be reduced*
1	To be completed at the end of the chapter
2	
3	
4	
5	

ANALYSING THE NATURE OF YOUR INCOMING STRESS

Consider the sources of stress that you have identified; which of the following boxes do you feel they come from?

Nature of stress	*Controllable*	*Not controllable (but potentially limitable)*
External	Attempting too many activities Too many high-stress activities, e.g. competitive or with deadlines or with potential to fail	Illness/death Family problems Money problems Accidents Major changes or problems at work
Internal	Poor time-management techniques, e.g. procrastination, lack of organization, leaving jobs unfinished, doing several jobs at once, untidy desk or office Attitude	Personality: you generate your own internal stresses because of negative thoughts, e.g. worry, anger, impatience, fear or insecurity These are controlled to a large extent by your personality driver (see next section)

Source of stress

Controllable stress: you can choose to reduce the amount of incoming stress if your ability to cope is not sufficient, and you can learn to improve your habits so as not to generate your own internal stresses; the rest of this chapter will show you how to do this.

Uncontrollable stress: you can reduce the *effects* of this stress by using time management techniques such as planning, lists and assertiveness, and by taking steps to reduce the effects of your personality driver.

Exercise:
Here are some of the controllable time-management-related causes of stress. How many of them do you have?

❑ Unpleasant jobs hanging over you

Overwork:
❑ trying to fit too much in, and feeling that you are doing none of it properly
❑ not taking enough physical rest or mental relaxation

❑ Doing a task that you know you shouldn't be, or that you don't really agree with, because you didn't say no

❑ General feeling of not tackling the big issues because all your time and energy is used on the small problems

❑ Multi-tasking: doing more than one job at a time

❑ Interruptions when you are in a hurry to finish a job

❑ Problems in the back of your mind when you are attempting to relax

❑ Deadlines coming up – uncertainty about whether they will be achieved

❑ Bursts of panic activity when everything hits at once

❑   Chatty people when you are busy

❑   Being late and not being able to do anything about it (e.g. stuck in traffic or waiting for the photocopier)

  Uneasy feeling of not achieving goals
❑   in life
❑   at work

❑   Job list getting longer and longer every day – not enough time in a day to get it all done

❑   Not as physically fit as you should be

Now look back over the boxes you have ticked: what can you do to reduce these causes of stress, in terms of improving your time management? If after reading this chapter you don't have the answers, they are given in Appendix 2.

Next we will look at one of the major internal causes of stress: your personality driver.

PERSONALITY DRIVERS AS SOURCES OF INTERNAL STRESS

We all have varying amounts of one or more of the following five drivers, which are seated deep in our subconscious minds and which control most of our thoughts and actions:

■   hurry up
■   please others
■   be perfect
■   try hard
■   be strong.

These drivers appear to be passed down from parents to their small children. In their first few years of life children interpret the events around them to form a view of how the world works and how to behave.

Driver	*Caused when young children are told:*
Hurry up	'There isn't time to play with you'
Please others	'You must not be selfish', 'You must share'
Be perfect	'You made a small mistake and that's bad'
Try hard	'You failed and it was your own fault'
Be strong	'Don't cry', 'Only babies cry'

These are all major psychological events when we are small, and if overdone can have a lasting impact on our adult behaviour patterns. All five drivers are linked to stress, and the first three have a dramatic effect on time management. The following sections are designed to help you recognize your own driver (and you may have more than one!) and to help you reduce its effects. You may wish to ask someone who knows you well to read each section and to tell you whether you have the driver.

Hurry up

The effect of this driver is to make you very conscious of time, to the point where you try to fit too much in, don't have time to prepare or finish off properly, don't have time for box 3 activities (planning for the future) and don't have time to enjoy the present (sometimes known as not 'taking time to smell the roses'). It's constantly 'OK, done that, what's next?' You get a lot done, but at the cost of high stress and low quality of life. You are impatient with pedantic people who pull you up on points of detail. You hate being kept waiting. You often do several things at once. You find it difficult to focus all your attention on your children, and may find yourself saying to them 'I haven't got time for that now' (which will pass on your driver to them). As a manager you may find that you become impatient with your team and have a tendency not to spend enough time on one-to-one coaching and involving.

If this is your driver, you could try to reduce its effect by deliberately slowing down; take up a restful sport like fishing or golf and make sure you take your time at it. Make sure you take time to sit and think. Go for regular walks and consciously admire the beauty of nature. Ask others to let you know if you're 'hurrying up'.

Please others

The effect of this driver is to make you friendly and caring to the point where you put the priorities of others before your own. This becomes a problem when you become frustrated that you are not achieving the progress that you would like, and when however much time you spend on other people you still feel guilty that you're not doing enough for them. Whatever compliments they give you, you always have the nagging feeling that you are asking them for too many favours, or even that they may not really like you.

Like the other drivers, 'please others' can never be satisfied by your *trying* to satisfy it. The best approach is to reduce its strength by conscious self-talk: 'Other people are responsible for their own lives', 'I don't have to worry what others think about me', 'I can make my own decisions', 'My own objectives are important', 'Other people like me'. If you feel extremely uncomfortable saying these sentences out loud, then you have this driver and you therefore *need* to say them!

Be perfect

Fear of making mistakes will make you thorough, but often *too* much of a perfectionist. You can't do everything perfectly! Some jobs aren't *worth* doing perfectly! But this driver will make you unable to let go, and a blemish, whether it's a spelling mistake in a memo or a scratch on a car, will ruin the whole thing for you. You may feel that others try to rush you or that their statements are too general to be useful. Your statements are carefully worded, and may often include subclauses, where appropriate and relevant, and numbered lists to give (1) structure, (2) clarity and (3) improved retention in the listener. You may tend to procrastinate because you don't have all of the information; you may be easily distracted by unfinished details on other work; you may find it hard to delegate because no one else does the job as carefully as you feel it should be done.

To fight against this driver (which, like all the others, has its strengths but is a problem when it gets out of hand) you need consciously to relax on the details. Force yourself to let other people do the work, even with mistakes. Force yourself to let it go when it's near enough finished. Say to yourself 'That detail does not matter. I don't mind. I am thinking about bigger things'. Remember that 80 per cent of your results come from 20 per cent of your time, and one of the reasons for the other 80 per cent being relatively unproductive could be that you spend too long on getting the details exactly right. Are there other tasks which are more important that are not even being started? Try working with a 'hurry up' person, and try to keep up with their generalizations without getting held back on the detail. They have their faults, but you can learn from them.

Try hard

The biggest sign of this driver is guilt. You feel that any failures are your fault – if only you'd worked a bit harder or been a bit cleverer. Although you are hardworking it never seems to be enough. Do you sometimes use the phrase 'if only . . .'? Worry is another sign of this driver; whereas regret is negativity aimed at the *past*, worry is negativity aimed at the *future*. Sometimes you plan for failure by saying 'Well, I'll try . . .', which means 'I'll try but I'll probably fail'. Are you good at spotting the possible pitfalls in a plan, to the point where you dwell on them? If you think about them enough they will probably happen, and a risk with the 'try hard' driver is that it will discourage you from really committing yourself to succeeding.

To fight this driver you need to focus on your successes. Think 'I did that well, and I can succeed at other things too.' Visualize yourself succeeding before you begin. Banish negative thoughts about the past or the future, forcing them out by replacing them with positive ones. If you do fail, say to yourself: 'What can I learn from this experience, so that I can succeed next time?' Then visualize yourself succeeding next time. You could say out loud 'I like myself' while looking in the mirror each morning. This is an excellent self-esteem builder and quickly changes from feeling very strange to feeling good. Try it for a week! Remember, it's not your fault that you have this driver, it's purely a result of your upbringing, and you have the power to change it if you wish.

Be strong

This driver prevents you showing your emotions. Instead you bottle them up, perhaps having the occasional outburst, or perhaps never revealing what you really think. Clearly this will add to your stress level and can lead to strained relationships. If you are unable to tell your children you love them, they too will grow up with the 'be strong' driver. Hopefully they will still know that you do love them, perhaps by your actions, but they too will be unable to say it. At work you will have difficulty giving praise – a common management failing. You will be calm in a crisis, but will find it hard to enjoy good situations – you won't *want* to smell the roses. Many 'be strong' people have to have a few drinks before they can enjoy themselves. Some use sport or music as an emotional outlet, but these are not a substitute for close relationships, which are the major source of happiness.

To fight this driver you need consciously to show your emotions. Force yourself to thank people, make a conscious effort to praise your children, and then go for the big one – tell your partner that you love them. If there is a person who is particularly difficult to open up to, visualize yourself doing so. Think about who you know who is difficult to talk to; for example, could you say to your mother or father that they have been a good parent? Practice thanking members of your team for a job well done – make sure you catch every one of them doing something *right* at least once a month.

There is a link between the personality drivers and the four personality types discussed in chapter 7, with the 'be perfect' and 'hurry up' drivers on the horizontal 'time' axis, and 'be strong' and 'please others' on the vertical 'people' axis. The following diagram may help you to decide what personality type you are and/or to discover which drivers you are prone to:

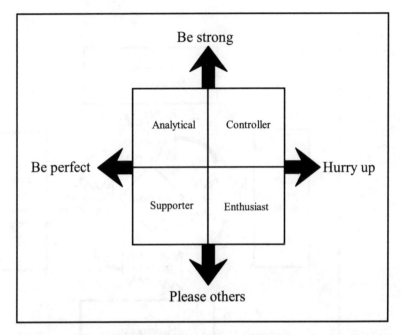

If we refer to the model of quality of life from chapter 2, it is clear that these drivers can interfere with quality of life in the following ways:

■ 'Hurry up' prevents us from enjoying peace of mind – there is always one more thing to do. It also affects happiness and intimacy because of the inability to relax.

■ 'Please others' can prevent us using our time on our own objectives and achieving the results we want. It can also affect our peace of mind, as it makes us worry about whether other people like us.

■ 'Be perfect' can detract from the ability to live in the here and now and experience fun. There will always be imperfections: the trick is not to focus on them. 'Be perfect' can also detract from the satisfaction of achievements for the same reason.

■ 'Try hard' affects all of the areas by striking at the self-image in the centre – expecting to fail will reduce achievement, fun, happiness and peace of mind.

■ 'Be strong' is the barrier to intimacy and therefore reduces the happiness to be gained from relationships, and also tends to reduce the ability to let go and have fun (and show it).

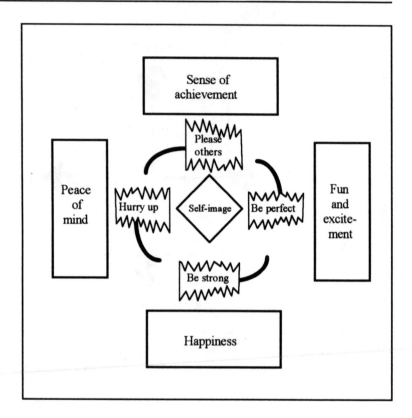

SUMMING UP DRIVERS

■ What is your main driver?

■ What others do you have?

Do you agree that although they have advantages they must not be allowed to rule your life?

■ Advantages of your drivers:

■ Disadvantages:

■ What actions will you take as a result of reading this section?

YOUR ABILITY TO COPE

We have seen how stress comes from external and internal sources, some being more controllable than others. Your ability to cope with stress needs to exceed the amount of stress you have coming in to you. Your ability to cope comes from three areas.

Personality

Your personality is both a *source* of stress, as we have seen with the five drivers, and a factor in your *ability to cope* with stress. You cannot change your personality but if you want to you *can* change the behaviour that results from it, by using the self-talk techniques already discussed in chapter 2. However, much easier ways to increase your ability to cope with stress are to increase your experience and to improve your techniques.

Past experience

Experience of *similar events* in the past affects both our confidence and our skills. For example, moving house does not feel stressful if you do it every year or two, but to uproot after twenty years is a major event. In management terms, training – for example simulations and role-playing – can be a quicker route than real experience.

Past experience of *larger stresses* also affects our ability to handle stress. An extreme example is where a close brush with death (or a day's rock climbing!) puts everyday worries into perspective.

Personally I wouldn't recommend anything really dangerous but I *would* recommend an activity like rock climbing as a way to increase your ability to handle stressful situations.

Techniques

The quickest and most significant way to improve your ability to cope with stress is by the time-management techniques outlined in the final section of this chapter and in the rest of this book.

Shown below is a situation where your stress level is under control, although there is not a particularly large safety margin.

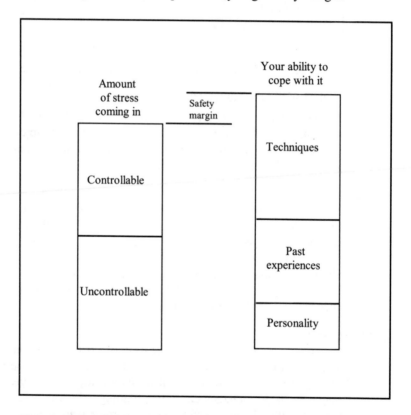

If the uncontrollable stress increases – say with insecurity at work or marriage problems at home – your ability to cope may not be enough. Similarly, in the example shown there is not much scope for taking on additional stressful activities. But at least the situation is under control.

The next diagram shows a situation where the stress levels are too high.

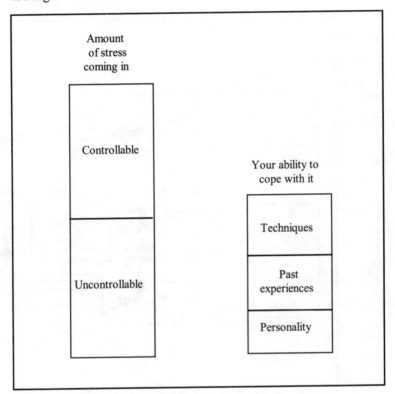

The point at which the balance is exceeded will be different for everyone. We all have different personalities, different past experience and differing skill levels at coping with problems. (The changeover point is not sudden, but performance gradually declines as the input starts to exceed the ability to cope.) There is also a link between the amount of stress you are experiencing and your ability to handle it. The imbalance shown above could easily result in further-reduced ability to cope, as time-management techniques are abandoned in panic and past experience is forgotten, resulting in a downward spiral.

This tendency to spiral is exacerbated by the fact that the symptoms of stress are often the causes of even more stress; for example, if you drink more when under stress your ability to perform will be impaired, adding to your stress and therefore your drinking. The same with sleeping badly, keeping a tidy desk, etc. (see below).

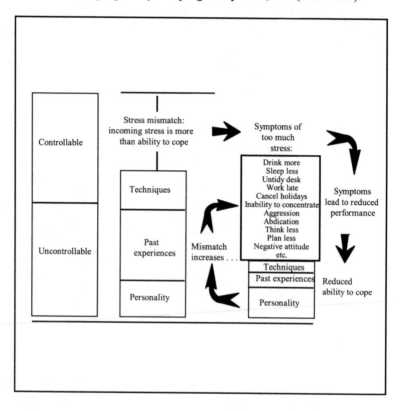

If your stress level is beyond this balance point your options are

■ to reduce the amount of stress coming in (if it is avoidable)
■ to increase your capacity for handling it.

YOUR STRESS LEVEL DURING THE DAY

Your stress level varies during the day, and a key symptom is the level of stress still remaining when you are attempting to go to sleep. The graphs below show an ideal daily stress curve, and then a curve for someone who is suffering from excess stress at work. In the first graph, you have enough time to get into your optimum working band before work (perhaps a walk before work or some reading) and you stay in your optimum band for your whole day at work. In the evening you still have the energy to be in the optimum band for most of the time, but towards the end of the evening you relax enough to be able to go to sleep easily.

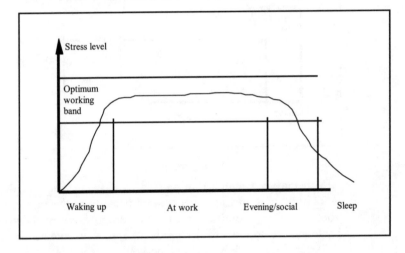

In the next graph there are some problems. The morning is a shock – there is less time between waking up and going to work, so you are not yet fully functional when you reach work. You rushed to get there, either as a consequence of not getting up early enough (perhaps because of not getting enough sleep) or because you are starting work early in order to work long hours. During the day your stress level rises to a high level at which you are not operating as effectively as you could be: perhaps you find yourself making emotional decisions, not listening to others, not allocating time to important subjects, not planning, or perhaps forgetting things or becoming irritable or aggressive. Then, during the evening you are not slowing down enough, so although you are in your optimum zone in the evening you fail to reach a relaxed state for sleep. You keep a pad by the bed and switch the light on again to write down brilliant ideas for work. You go to sleep thinking about work, and after a night of dreaming about work you awake, not refreshed, to start the cycle over again.

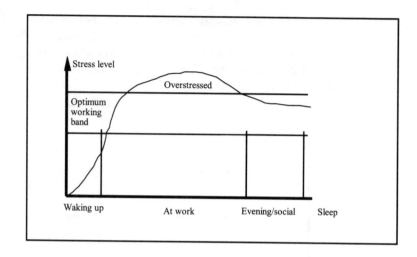

You may not match this pattern exactly: maybe you drive to work and arrive already overstressed because of the traffic; maybe you stay at work until after you have dropped out of the effective band and are no longer fully productive, so you have no energy left for your life outside work; maybe you never get into the effective band on some days! The question is, what does your graph look like and should you take steps to change it? Take a moment to draw it in:

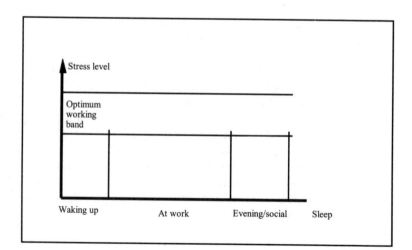

In the above graphs there is an optimum working band, within which you are functioning effectively. Below it you are bored or asleep, and above it you are under too much stress to be as creative or as effective as you could be. Your rate of achievement is reduced, as is your quality of life. In the next section we will explore this optimum band in more depth. Is it really a band, or just an ideal point above or below which your performance is less good? What governs its position?

YOUR IDEAL STRESS LEVEL

As already discussed, individuals have differing capabilities for coping with stress. Their 'resilience' will affect where each person's ideal point is. But for all of us there *will be* an ideal point. In fact, there is an ideal point for maximum achievement of results and there is another point where your quality of life is optimized. Above and below the ideal stress points your performance is reduced. If you were to draw graphs of these they would probably look roughly like this:

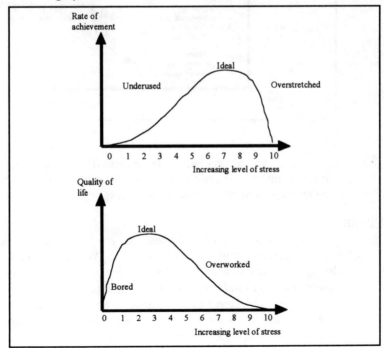

As you can see, your ideal point from the achievement-of-results point of view is at a higher stress level than the ideal point for quality of life. This means that to be higher than your maximum achievement point or lower than the ideal quality-of-life point is certainly unwise, but where to be in the trade-off region between them is a matter of personal choice. Do you want to maximize the current quality of your life or do you want to work harder now for, hopefully, better quality of life in the future?

This dilemma is shown in the next diagram, which has combined the above two graphs and taken out the stress axis, thus relating *rate of achievement* directly to *quality of life*:

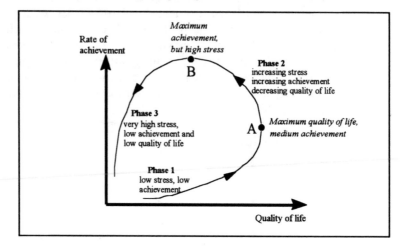

In reality you are stationary somewhere on the above line, but to illustrate the various positions you might occupy, let's imagine that you take a tour along the line of increasing stress.

Phase 1

Initially your activity rate is so low that you are not achieving much and not deriving much satisfaction either. You are a couch potato, living in the low achievement/low quality of life section of the diagram, and you could *achieve more* (defined as making progress towards any objectives that *you* care to select) *and* improve your quality of life by moving your activity level up a gear. A good start would be to find some objectives that excite you.

To be anywhere in the first phase cannot be sensible, because for any point in the first phase, shown as point C in the next diagram, you could move up vertically to point D and achieve much more for the same quality of life.

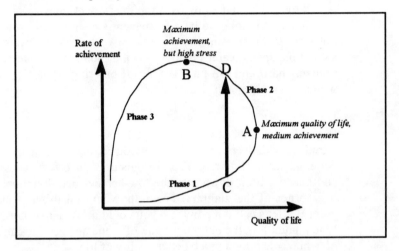

If you are at point A you are either on holiday or living a life which has a similar feel. Your quality of life is high and your rate of achievement is reasonable, in that you are doing enough to keep yourself stimulated. At point A your quality of life is maximized, though you could be achieving more.

Phase 2

After point A you enter the trade-off zone, which (including the end-points A and B) is the optimum place to be. As you move up the line from A towards B you are sacrificing *quality of life now* for achievement and (hopefully) *future* quality of life. This is a trade-off that you must judge according to your own personality, goals and circumstances.

Maybe you feel that quality of life right now is what you should be aiming for, and this is more important than ambition for the future. Or maybe you feel that you want to be at your maximum achievement peak now in order to build results for the future. The difficulty with the second strategy is that although quality of life in the future is likely to require some sort of work now, and therefore a temporary sacrifice of quality of life, it won't *necessarily* follow. So there is a risk. If you are at point B, you should make sure that your long-term plan is a good one. At B you are at your most pro- ductive, but you are paying a price. You are not taking the time to 'smell the roses' and enjoy living in the present. Staying at point B is probably not going to be a permanent strategy, since you would not want to finish your life without harvesting your rewards with some time spent nearer point A. Also, at point B you are working yourself hard and are on the edge of entering phase 3, the area which is not physically sustainable.

Phase 3

Beyond point B the stress level is too high. Your effectiveness starts to reduce with overwork and over-tiredness, and your quality of life continues to decline too. You are outside your effectiveness band and heading back down into the low-achievement/low quality-of- life corner of the diagram. From anywhere on this line beyond point B – let's call it a point E – you could move across horizontal- ly to a point F in the optimum trade-off zone and get the same level of achievement for a much better quality of life.

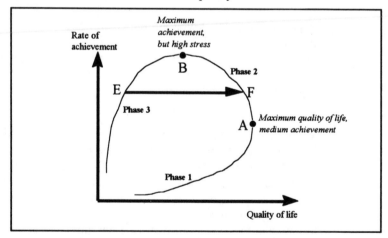

Phase 3 is clearly not the place to be. So why would anyone be here? Perhaps because the incoming stress levels are not control- lable and the techniques for coping are not sufficient; or because the delusion is that performance is not affected and that the results from all the work will lead to future quality of life. If this is you, then you need to take action.

Moving back from phase 3 into the optimum trade-off area, or moving within the trade-off area towards point A (your optimum quality of life), means reducing your stress level. In the next section we will look at ways to achieve this.

APPROACHES FOR REDUCING YOUR CURRENT STRESS LEVEL

So far we have seen how stress shows itself in mental and physical signs, and how stress comes partly from external sources but is also partly internally generated, especially by our personality drivers. We have seen how some sources of stress are beyond our control but many are controllable. We have seen how there is an internal balance between the amount of stress coming in and the amount we can cope with. Our ability to cope is affected by our personality, our previous experience of similar or worse situations, and the techniques we use to manage ourselves. Our resulting stress level varies during the day, and should ideally be in a band between our optimum quality of life and our maximum rate of achievement – below the optimum quality of life is a waste of ability, and above the maximum rate of achievement is likely to lead to a downward spiral of reduced performance. The choice of where exactly to be on the sliding scale between achievement and quality of life is a personal decision.

Exercise:
It is possible that after thinking about the above ideas you have decided to reduce your stress level, in which case this final section summarizes your options. As you read the following checklist, mark any items that you feel would help you.

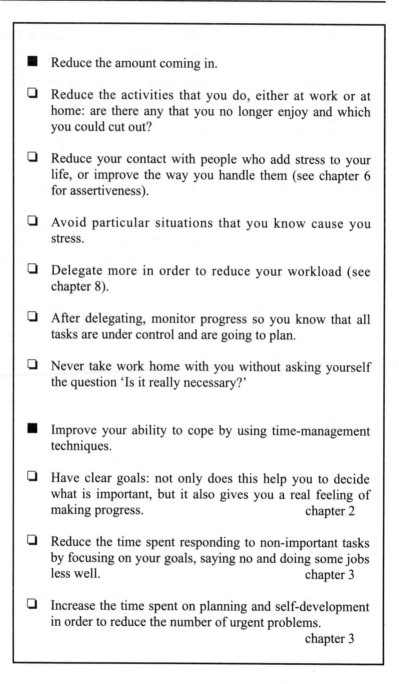

■ Reduce the amount coming in.

❏ Reduce the activities that you do, either at work or at home: are there any that you no longer enjoy and which you could cut out?

❏ Reduce your contact with people who add stress to your life, or improve the way you handle them (see chapter 6 for assertiveness).

❏ Avoid particular situations that you know cause you stress.

❏ Delegate more in order to reduce your workload (see chapter 8).

❏ After delegating, monitor progress so you know that all tasks are under control and are going to plan.

❏ Never take work home with you without asking yourself the question 'Is it really necessary?'

■ Improve your ability to cope by using time-management techniques.

❏ Have clear goals: not only does this help you to decide what is important, but it also gives you a real feeling of making progress.   chapter 2

❏ Reduce the time spent responding to non-important tasks by focusing on your goals, saying no and doing some jobs less well.   chapter 3

❏ Increase the time spent on planning and self-development in order to reduce the number of urgent problems.
                                    chapter 3

❑ Take action rather than procrastinating.   chapter 4

❑ Get all the facts rather than speculating and worrying.

Fear of the unknown and pessimism about the future can be reduced by getting the facts. If you let fear of bad news prevent you facing up to issues you will be living with stress and the issue is unlikely to go away.

❑ Practise assertiveness as a substitute for submission.
                                                          chapter 6

❑ Practise assertiveness as a substitute for aggression.
                                                          chapter 6

❑ Think: 'No one else has the right to make me angry – I decide that.'   chapter 6

❑ Control interruptions.   chapter 6

❑ Know your own stress symptoms.   chapter 9

❑ Keep your desk tidy.   chapter 10

❑ Write everything down, especially jobs to do and problems that need attention.   chapter 10

❑ Have a clear plan for tomorrow (a jobs-to-do-list).
                                                          chapter 10

❑ Realize that a perfectly dovetailed day with 100 per cent of the time allocated before it starts is a recipe for lateness and stress. Leave some space for unspecified events which will probably crop up, and use this for box 3 (non-urgent but important) tasks if the events don't crop up.

❑ Write a list of all the problems and their worst possible outcomes, listing the possible action choices.

■ Improve your ability to cope, *as a person.*

Physical improvements:

❑ Spend twenty minutes every other day on fitness – there is a link between the effective functioning of your body and the effective functioning of your mind.

❑ Eat well and sensibly.

❑ Reduce caffeine intake, e.g. coffee, tea, etc.

❑ Cut back on drinking and give up smoking.

❑ Use 'release' sports, like squash, cycling or weight training.

❑ Try exciting/frightening sports like rock climbing, which help put small worries into context.

❑ Take up relaxing activities like fishing or walking.

❑ Organize a peaceful 'home base' where you can relax and think; for example, a room in your house which is comfortable, organized, calm, tidy – whatever works for you.

❑ Get enough sleep.

Getting your close relationships right:

❑ Improve the balance of home and work (see chapter 1).

❑ Spend enough time with people who are important to you.

❑ Be open in your relationships, expressing feelings and giving sincere compliments. Learn to overcome your 'be strong' driver if necessary.

❏ Practise listening and showing that you have understood.

❏ Talk frankly to your boss about your objectives and progress.

Enlist the help and support of others:

❏ Ask for advice.

❏ Listen to advice and weigh it up impartially before judging it.

❏ Take the advice, act on it and thank the provider for it.

Self-development:

❏ Read (develop a list of books to investigate by checking the bibliographies of books you found useful).

❏ Try some training: learn from experts.

❏ Associate with and learn from people who you would like to emulate – who would you choose as a role model, at work and outside work? How can you get to spend some time with them?

❏ Use self-talk to strengthen your weaknesses.

❏ Resist your internal personality drivers.

Positive thought:

❏ Let go of the past: grudges and regret are like little coiled springs in your head which take mental effort to maintain, adding stress and reducing your ability to be positive and make progress.

❏ Consciously enjoy the present – say to yourself 'This is great!', 'This is the life!', 'This is an adventure!' Saying these words, either in your head or, preferably, out loud, will influence your subconscious and make them true for you (see chapter 2 for more details).

❏ Practise seeing problems as opportunities.

❏ Avoid dwelling on negative possibilities – if you think about them enough, they'll probably happen!

❏ Visualize good outcomes in situations – consciously say to yourself 'This will be easy', or 'I will do well' or 'They will do exactly what I want'. This is the exact opposite of worrying, which is visualizing the outcome that you *don't* want.

❏ Visualize a good long-term future for yourself. What image of yourself in five years time do you have at the back of your mind? Is it a good one? Is it detailed? Many people just have a vague feeling of unease which they don't want to think about. Remember that you get what you picture.

Now please turn back to the table you filled in earlier in this chapter, where you listed in the left-hand column your top five causes of stress. You can now develop a plan for the methods you will use to reduce these.

10 Efficient systems: what should you do every day?

In the introduction I suggested that an efficient daily system is the foundation of any successful person's life.

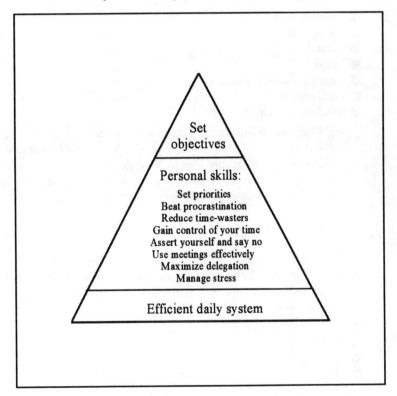

Set
objectives

Personal skills:

Set priorities
Beat procrastination
Reduce time-wasters
Gain control of your time
Assert yourself and say no
Use meetings effectively
Maximize delegation
Manage stress

Efficient daily system

Without goals there is no point in being efficient: you will travel very fast, but to where? With goals but without an efficient system, you won't make any progress. Your personal organization system must therefore

- encourage you to spend time on activities that lead to long-term progress
- give an overview for planning
- prevent lateness and forgetfulness
- save time when tasks repeat themselves
- reduce stress
- allow space for fun and spontaneity.

So what should an efficient daily system look like? In this final chapter we will look at the ideal personal organization system under the following headings:

- master actions list
- daily jobs-to-do list
- diary
- desk
- image: the importance of the above
- daily routine
- making it happen.

Everyone is different, in terms of character, job and the way they live their life, so one Filofax-type system cannot be prescribed for everyone. Some people like to have detailed lists and plans, while others prefer slips of paper or a small notebook. However, there are three features that every efficient system must have.

MASTER ACTIONS LIST

This is quite simply a single list of every job that you have got to do, all written down in one place. Do you have this? In my experience, only about one person in twenty has such a list.

Why don't most people have one?

- never thought about it
- can't be bothered
- lack of self-discipline
- fear that the list will be too long to cope with.

What will happen if you don't have one?

- stress: you will have an uneasy feeling that there are lots of things you probably should be doing

- you will forget things
- you will find it easy to procrastinate
- you won't be able to prioritize
- you won't be able to stand back to review progress and plan ahead.

Considering that it will take you about five minutes to write and then less than a minute a day to maintain, I am sure that you will agree that this is worth doing! So, are *you* going to do one? Today?

The best format for your master list is:

- any order
- every job, big or small
- written on one piece of paper
- or in your diary
- or on a collection of cards
- or on pages in a ring file, either A4 or small
- or listed on a computer or computerized diary.

In order to capture everything without forgetting it you should always carry a pen and paper with you. You can then write down an idea or something you are asked to do and get straight back to concentrating on what you were doing. It sounds simple, but do you do it?

From your master list you can then extract the jobs that you will do each day, based on whether the jobs are urgent and also whether they are important. As discussed in detail in chapter 3, the ideal mix is to cover all the urgent ones while still fitting in some of the non-urgent but *important* ones. This will enable you to stay ahead of the game and achieve your desired quality of life in the longer term.

DAILY JOBS-TO-DO LIST

This has been described by other time management writers as the single biggest aid to getting more done in a day. This is because it makes you focus on what you are going to get done, and helps you to avoid wasting time. It is a great way of reducing procrastination, it helps you plan your day and it acts as a reward when you cross out each job and then, on a good day, finish the list completely!

Writing a jobs-to-do list reduces stress by

- making sure you have a reassuring plan for tomorrow rather than an uncertain fog
- releasing your mind from having to remember all the tasks.

Write your jobs-to-do list the evening before. For work tasks, you should write it just before going home and leave it on your desk. This tells your subconscious that tomorrow is well planned and organized, and that you are leaving all thoughts of work behind when you go home. Your subconscious will prepare you for whatever you are planning to do tomorrow, so you will perform better when the time comes. The list also sets your subconscious quietly working on some of the problems, while you sleep or do other work. Answers to problems will sometimes pop into your mind just before you need them. You will find that writing the list the evening before makes it much easier to commit yourself to doing the unpleasant tasks that you would normally avoid with 'I'm too busy' or 'I don't have quite enough information yet'. If you leave it until the next morning you may easily be sidetracked by an urgent problem as soon as you arrive at work, and then you will not get around to writing your list. So write it the evening before.

Why is the master list not enough to work from? Why is it necessary to write a new, extra little list each day? The answer is that if you try to work from your master list,

- you will 'cherry pick', taking the best jobs and leaving the unpleasant ones
- you will feel depressed because you never finish the master list
- it's unwieldy and you might even lose it.

What should your daily list look like?

- ten items at the most
- written on a small piece of paper
- or written in your diary
- always with you
- added to as the day continues
- crossed out as you go.

Some people like to sort jobs into the following categories:

- must do (stay on until finished)
- should do (feel guilty if not done)
- might do (if the day turns out to be a quiet one).

Others like to mark the important ones with a star, or write the jobs in order of urgency. This is a matter of personal preference, and I would not like to discourage you from keeping a daily list by prescribing it in too much detail and making it too much effort. However, if you can, I do recommend writing the jobs in the order in which you are planning to do them. This makes you less likely to leave the difficult ones until it is too late.

One manager I know puts an easy job at the top of his list, to get himself going in the morning, and then the worst job of the day second. He likes to get this out of the way early rather than think about it all day. Another manager has a small home-made pad with the dates of every day already written on the top of each consecutive page. This means that every day (in the evening) she *has* to write the jobs list for the next day. Try making a pad like this for yourself: it works so well that within ten days you will be running out of urgent jobs to put in it! You will then be able to put the *important* ones in it.

It will take you less than five minutes per day to write your list for the following morning. I am sure you will agree that this is time well spent. So, are *you* going to do one? Today?

DIARY

Without a diary you cannot plan ahead and you cannot hope to remember appointments or be on time. Your diary should be small enough to be always with you and contain work and home appointments. When you are at one place you need to know when your next appointment is at the other place; separating your work and home diaries will increase your stress level as your brain will have to manage two identities.

It should also contain a note of what the next action on a project is to be. Each project should be like an unbroken chain, so if someone says they'll get back to you, or you are waiting for a letter, or there is a date when your next section of work is due, or you haven't got time to think about a problem today, write in your diary what the next action is, by whom, and write it in on the day when it is due. This reduces your stress level because that loose end is now taken care of and can be put out of your mind until it comes up. Other people will be amazed at your efficiency when you call them and say 'You promised it for today, how's it coming?' or 'There are two weeks until the deadline, shall we arrange that preparatory meeting for next week?'

You don't need a good memory, you just need to write the next action down in your diary. Never let the chain become broken until the job is finished!

You should leave numerous spaces in your diary. After your essential appointments have been entered in your diary, you can programme in some blocks of time for your important but non-urgent tasks. These may only be one or two blocks of half an hour each day, but they will encourage you to spend proactive time on the things that matter to you. Remember that an hour per day is equivalent to five solid weeks of work per year. Most box 2 (unimportant but urgent) interruptions can wait until after the half-hour block, but box 1 (urgent and important) interruptions will occasionally have to be done right away and ruin your allocated block. This is unavoidable, but at least most of your blocks will be achieved.

Make sure that 50 per cent of your diary is still unprogrammed each day, for all the box 2 (urgent but unimportant) problems that will certainly crop up. If you allow less than this, your day will be frantic and your stress level will be too high. Over-planning or over-management of time can be quite a stress-raiser, since the plans will not work out!

Your diary is the place to put all sorts of other information in, not just dates; for example, in my diary I have

- all my frequently used phone numbers
- some key addresses and postcodes
- maps of the country and a street map of my home area
- expense records
- stamps and costs of posting overseas/overweight in the UK
- useful numbers: National Insurance, driving licence and all bank/credit card numbers except PINs
- list of birthdays and other dates to remember
- list of what to remember to pack when going away (based on bitter experience of what I normally forget)
- information on key business contacts
- list of books to read, added to when people recommend one to me
- photo of my dog.

You don't have to have all these things, and you will probably add others, but the main points are the following:

- write everything down – you never know when you'll need it
- keep it all in one place, i.e. your diary, so you know where to look
- no more scraps of paper that you can't find
- it saves time and mental effort if you can look it up rather than trying to remember it
- downloading information on to paper frees up your mind to think.

Another important thing to remember is that your diary should be perpetual. To save starting again each year I use a small Filofax-type book with lots of loose pages after the diary for the above information. Another advantage of this is that around October I can put in some of next year's months, so I get the forward visibility I need. I prefer a week to two pages, plus a year on one pull-out triple page, but you can decide which to choose depending on how many jobs per day you need to plan and how far ahead your work horizon is.

Make sure your diary is secure. What if you lose it? This can be quite traumatic because, if properly used, a diary is such a valuable tool. I recommend that you

- never put it down anywhere other than back in your pocket or handbag
- don't leave it on your desk or in a hotel room
- never change your routine with it (putting it somewhere different, like giving it to your partner to look after, packing it in a different bag, etc.)
- don't put it in a bag with lots of other things, e.g. picnic bag, shopping bag
- photocopy key pages occasionally
- keep previous versions of phone lists etc.
- keep phone lists on computer and print out updated versions for putting into your diary – then you have the computer as back-up if the hard copy gets lost
- put your name and address on page one, with a message saying *please* return this diary, perhaps even with a small reward.

As mentioned before, your diary can also contain your long-term goals, your master actions list and, written in each day, your daily jobs-to-do list. If a job has a time when it needs to be done, or a best time to do it, then you should write it into your diary rather than your daily or master list. Similarly, if it is a small job you don't need to write it on your master list – it can go straight on to your daily list or into your diary. The master list is best for large jobs that cannot be completed in a day and for jobs for which you don't yet have a time of action. However, if these start to be procrastinated you can get a grip on them by putting them into your diary for a date in the future.

Apart from these three key parts of your paperwork system, there are some other aspects to your daily routine which are important, and these are discussed next.

DESK

Your desk is prime real estate, the most important two square yards in the world, so don't fill it up with old magazines you'll never read and papers you can't be bothered to file. Put these somewhere else, preferably in the bin but at least not in your top two square yards.

Personally, I don't advocate a completely clear desk, even when finishing for the day, but I do feel that there are certain rules that everyone should follow.

Pen and paper

Always have instant access to plenty of pens and rough paper. Otherwise you won't write things down when you should, and you are then on the slippery slope to chaos. I could never find a pen when I wanted one (where on earth do they go?), so I bought fifty and put them all around the house, in every room. This turned out to be just enough to saturate the house, so although I am down to my last ten they never quite disappear.

At work I write everything down. If my boss comes in and asks me to do something, I write it down. I then know I won't forget it, and can if necessary focus again on the job I was doing before the interruption. It also gives the signal that I *will* be taking action on the request. If I receive a phone call I take notes from the start so I don't forget their name or any points from the conversation, which could get long and complicated. What if you received another call straight after the first one and you didn't take notes during the first call? If I have an idea I write it down before I forget it again. All *actions* that I agree to do, or decide to do, are added either to my master actions list (if they are large and non-time specific) or to my diary (if I can decide immediately when I will do them). All *promises* made to me are written down in my diary, on the date when they are due.

Location

Make sure the view is conducive to thinking. Looking out of a window on to a busy road is too distracting, and facing a corridor is the same. We tend automatically to have our desk facing the door or direction of approach, as a defensive measure from our days as wild animals, but you should consider turning your desk away from (or sideways on to) areas of activity in order to aid concentration.

Empty your in-tray every day

Even if you just put it all in another pile somewhere, you need to keep your in-tray empty so that you can recognize new arrivals. If yesterday's incoming mail is buried by today's, you will have the stress of wondering if something in the pile is important or overdue. Also, others will have more faith that you will take action if your in-tray is under control. If people feel the need to put notes on your chair or on your computer keyboard then you have an image problem!

Ideally when you empty the in-tray you should do one of the following:

- read it and bin it
- read it and file it
- action it right now
- put it on one side to read more fully later
- put it on one side to action later
- put it one side to delegate later.

In other words, you make your decision on the next action immediately, and follow this by putting it into your system: write it on your daily list, or your master list, or in your diary to do at a known time in the future. It is then in the system, and the unbroken chain will pursue it until it gets finished.

Work on one job at a time

Trying to work on several jobs will mean you won't focus on any of them, they will all take longer, in terms of both lead-time and total hours worked, and you will have the extra stress of holding several jobs in your mind at once. Your subconscious can only show one picture at a time on its internal film projector.

Of course, there will be interruptions as you work on your important jobs, either from telephones or visitors, and these cannot be ignored. But after you have dealt with each interruption you should go back to your one important job. You should never have more than one important job being worked on at once. The other important jobs that are partly completed are not on your desk, they are in files, out of view. You open one of them and start it only after you have put away the one you have been working on.

Clutter

Never let 'dead' paper fill your desk area. If anything has not moved for more than two days, take it away somewhere else and keep the space clear. You will remember to do it because it is on your master list, and either in your diary or on your daily list too. But having it crowding you is adding stress to your life. Doesn't it feel like a marvellous relief, a weight off your mind, when you clear your desk top? This shows the amount of stress that the cluttered desk was putting on you.

Filing

When a piece of paper is to be filed, put the name of the destination file in the top corner and then put the paper in a tray. Then, when you file all the papers (every week or two) it is a quick and easy job to sort them into piles and file them. You don't need to read each one again and work out which file it should be in. If you have the luxury of a secretary you can delegate the physical sorting and putting away, while still controlling which file the papers go in and therefore being able to retrieve them yourself if you need to.

IMAGE: THE IMPORTANCE OF YOUR DESK AND YOUR PERSONAL ORGANIZATION SYSTEM

As well as being the foundation for achieving whatever results you want, your desk and your personal system will also be a major contribution to how others judge you. If promotion in your organization is one of your objectives, then here are a few things you will need to know.

Careers are decided 10 per cent on what you do, 20 per cent on who you know and 70 per cent on appearance.

Good appearance means being P-E-A-R shaped:

- positive attitude
- easy to work with
- appear to be in control
- reliable: do what you say, when you say you will.

Promotion, if it is your aim, depends largely on whether you can fulfil two criteria.

- You must be the sort of person your potential colleagues would like to work with: positive and easy to work with, 'a good team player'.

■ You must look as if you could do the job at the next level up, which means that you must be in control of your current job. In management, where delegation and teamwork are the major contributing factors to results rather than doing it all yourself, *personal competence* is more likely to make this difference than *technical competence*. If you are at the limit of your ability at your current level this will show in unreliability.

If your desk is tidy, you are always on time and you deliver the goods on time as promised, you will be a rare and valuable person. The right people will notice and want to work with you.

Even if corporate ambition is not your objective, you will probably want to be seen as reliable, easy to work with and positive by your friends and colleagues. I hope this book has given you enough ideas to move you into these categories!

DAILY ROUTINE

In the course of this chapter and in earlier chapters I mentioned a number of things that you need to do every day. Below is a list of everything that should be part of your daily routine if you want to live a satisfying and productive life.

Exercise:
As you read the following list, tick the ones you are already doing and then consider the gaps.

❑ Get up in plenty of time.

❑ Say: 'I feel great today.'

❑ Take time to read (something uplifting, not the papers).

❑ Take time to think and to review the plan for your day.

❑ Eat a healthy breakfast.

❑ Clear any unnecessary accumulations off your desk.

❑ During the day, get some exercise.

❑ Avoid negative people.

❑ Focus on your objectives or goals.

❑ Make sure you allocate some time for category 3 (important) tasks.

❑ Take time to smell the roses: savour some aspect of the day's experiences.

❑ Think about where time was wasted: what should you do next time?

❑ Finish work on time – do not regularly work long hours.

❑ Spend the maximum time on activities that you really enjoy.

❑ Avoid time-wasters, particularly TV.

❑ Avoid excessive eating or drinking.

❑ Spend quality time with your children, if you have any.

❑ Write your jobs-to-do list for tomorrow.

❑ Go to bed early enough to have sufficient sleep.

It takes about thirty days to make or break a habit, after which time it is no longer an effort to do, or avoid, the activity. Can you choose one of the above and keep it up for thirty days? Having established that particular success habit, you can then move on to another.

MAKING IT HAPPEN

Presumably you want to be a more efficient or organized person. I hope you have gained some new ideas while reading this book and have perhaps felt that you should do a few things differently. But will you actually do them differently? And if you do, how long will you keep it up? If you are not living your life even slightly differently in six months time, then my writing this book and your reading it will both have been a waste of time! So, here are some things you could do.

Action list

Flick through the book and compile a list of everything you would ideally like to do differently or better.

On the wall

Put this list on the wall, somewhere where you will see it often.

Reminder notes

Make small notices and put them around the house or your office, or hide them in places where they will surprise you.

We saw in chapter 2 how repetition is important for programming your goals into your subconscious. You can also use the repetition from reminder notices to

- remind yourself of your priorities
- reduce procrastination by whatever method you chose in chapter 4
- be more assertive when situations occur
- resist interruptions
- delegate more
- monitor and reduce stress
- control your personality driver (see chapter 9)
- keep your systems efficient.

How about putting a reminder notice for one of the above somewhere where you will see it occasionally, perhaps in your sock draw, or inside a kitchen cupboard, or in your car, or at the bottom of the washing basket or in one of the drawers of your filing cabinet? I have named my word processor disk with an inspirational reminder message, so that when I start up my PC in the morning it tells me the name of the disk and I am given a small jolt in the right direction. Some people have a tiny red dot above their desk, on a wall in their house, or in their car. The dot is a reminder to them of the personal goals which they have listed. Whenever they catch sight of the dot their subconscious is reminded of their goals. The advantage of the dot is that it means nothing to anybody else.

Reward yourself if you achieve any of your actions

For example, buy yourself some chocolate whenever you empty your filing tray or clear your desk. This sends a powerful message to your subconscious that the action is worth repeating.

Form the habit

See if you can keep up the new behaviour for thirty days – this is how long it takes to make a habit. Can you write a daily jobs-to-do list every day for thirty days? Can you read before breakfast for thirty days? Can you play with the children for an hour after work before watching the TV, for thirty consecutive days? Can you get some exercise every day for thirty days? Keep a chart on the wall and tick off the boxes. Remember, if you miss one you go back to the start!

Get a friend to help you

Appoint them as your official nagger. Ask them to ask you every day 'Have you got your jobs-to-do list today? Can I see it?' Get the friend to point out signs of stress or times when your internal driver is showing (being too perfect, being too rushed, etc.).

Pay in advance

Sign up for swimming classes or an aerobics class, and pay in advance so you are under some pressure to go.

Use your diary as a reminder

Write some reminders into your diary. Block in some time to clear your desk or go for a run. Write a note to yourself which you will discover in six months time saying 'How much TV are you watching?' or 'How much do you weigh?'

ACTION PLAN

■ Are you going to write a master actions list? Yes or no:

■ Are you going to write a jobs-to-do list every evening for the next day? Yes or no:

■ Improvements you can make to your diary:

■ Changes you will make to your desk:

■ Changes you plan to make to your daily routine:

■ How will you make your planned actions happen?

Remember,

you only get one life,

some of it is gone already,

but you can change the rest of it
and achieve anything you really want to.

Start now!

Appendix 1: answers to time-management symptoms questionnaire

Do you remember the list of symptoms in chapter 1? Let's now make sure that we have answers to each of them. You may wish to cover the page with a sheet of paper and reveal each answer only once you have thought about the methods you could use.

Unable to name one ambitious life goal without needing to think about it first.

Answer:
- ❏ from chapter 2 you will have done some thinking about where you want your future life to go – select the top goal from your list
- ❏ write this on a card and keep the card in your wallet or on your person at all times
- ❏ look at it every day – it *will* happen!

Large number of short-term problems means that long-term objectives don't get the time that they deserve.

Answer:
- ❏ write them all down
- ❏ look at them ruthlessly: how many are box 4 jobs?
- ❏ spend more time on box 3 jobs

Feeling pressured by unpleasant jobs still not done.

Answer:
- ❑ do the worst jobs first
- ❑ write a list of them and get them done
- ❑ see the chapters on stress (chapter 9) and procrastination (chapter 4) for more details

Unpleasant tasks postponed too many times.

Answer:
- ❑ have a master list of all of them
- ❑ work through your jobs-to-do list in order
- ❑ block in time when you will do them
- ❑ see chapter 4 for more ideas

Needing the pressure of the deadline to make you get round to doing the job.

Answer:
- ❑ assign blocks of time in your diary, or set a date when you will do it
- ❑ tell others about this date
- ❑ see chapter 4

Doing a job less well due to a last-minute rush.

Answer:
- ❑ plan ahead – more time spent on box 3, see chapter 3
- ❑ less procrastinating: see chapter 4

At the end of some days, wondering where all the time went.

Answer:
- ❑ use a jobs-to-do list and cross them off as you go
- ❑ allocate blocks in your diary for important jobs
- ❑ monitor progress towards your goals

Making the same mistake more than once.

Answer:
- ❏ use systems like checklists wherever possible
- ❏ improve your systems so that mistakes *cannot* be repeated

Saying yes and then regretting it later.

Answer:
- ❏ have objectives that you believe in, and focus on them
- ❏ use the four-step process for saying no assertively yet politely

Work controls you rather than you controlling it.

Answer:
- ❏ spend more time on category 3 tasks (planning) and therefore reduce the time spent fire-fighting; if this sounds too hard, read chapter 3 again!
- ❏ analyse your time-wasters (see chapter 5)
- ❏ use a daily jobs-to-do list to help you focus on what needs to be done
- ❏ resist interruptions, using ideas from chapter 6

Thinking about work problems at home.

Answer:
- ❏ write them all down
- ❏ reduce stress at work by planning
- ❏ see chapter 9 for more details

Not sure what you will achieve tomorrow.

Answer:
- ❏ have clear objectives
- ❏ have a jobs-to-do list already written out the evening before
- ❏ have time blocked in for important tasks

Untidy desk; some jobs have been on it for more than a week.

Answer:
- ❑ no dead areas on your desk
- ❑ clear it all off once a week
- ❑ work on only one job at a time
- ❑ keep a box for papers which you can 'almost' throw away; empty this box into the bin occasionally

Forgetting important things/remembering them too late.

Answer:
- ❑ keep a master jobs list
- ❑ write everything down
- ❑ keep an unbroken chain on each task: 'next action' goes into diary

Missing deadlines.

Answer:
- ❑ write everything down
- ❑ break large tasks down into subtasks, and put dates on these so they become progress milestones in your diary

Not finishing all the jobs on your jobs-to-do list each day.

Answer:
- ❑ use only a short daily jobs-to-do list
- ❑ keep a longer master list of all jobs that need to be done, some time
- ❑ do the daily-list jobs in the order of the list
- ❑ use the methods suggested in chapter 6 for reducing and controlling interruptions

— *Appendix 2: answers to time-management-related stress questionnaire*

In chapter 9 you identified some of the time-management-related causes of stress in your life. Many of the answers will have been clear as soon as you identified the source of the stress, and all of them are described in other chapters of this book. Here they are, summarized.

■ Unpleasant jobs hanging over you.

Chapter 4 gives twenty-five ideas on how you can overcome your tendency to procrastinate.

■ Overwork: trying to fit too much in, and feeling that you are doing none of it properly.

This is a question of prioritizing: which of your activities are *really* important to you, and which are merely urgent because they are important to someone else (chapter 3). Use a daily jobs-to-do list to help you focus on the important jobs (chapter 10). You may need to let go of your 'be perfect' driver, if you have one (as discussed in chapter 9). You should also consider delegating more (chapter 8) or saying no more often (chapter 6).

■ Overwork: not taking enough physical rest or mental relaxation.

This is again a question of prioritizing: you could book some time with yourself in your diary or include 'thinking time' on your daily list of things to do. The section in chapter 10 on 'Making it happen' contains some ideas on how you can make changes become part of the routine of your daily life.

■ Doing a task that you know you shouldn't, or that you don't really agree with, because you didn't say no.

See chapter 6 for saying no. If you *do* decide to do a job that you feel is unimportant, then make sure you spend the minimum time on it.

■ General feeling of not tackling the big issues because all your time and energy is used on the small problems.

You probably know what the big issues are, so the next step is to break them down into chunks and schedule these in your diary or on your daily jobs list. You may also need to get more assertive over the box 2 tasks that are clogging up your time, either by saying no or by doing them less well.

■ Multi-tasking: doing more than one job at a time.

Clear your desk (chapter 10), use a daily jobs list with the items numbered in the order that you will do them (chapter 10), and control interruptions (chapter 6). Remember that dealing with unavoidable interruptions and then returning to the one important job again is OK and is not the same as trying to do two important jobs at once. Write down agreed actions before returning to the main task.

■ Interruptions when you are in a hurry to finish a job.

See chapter 6 for strategies for handling interruptions. This problem could also be a sign that you have left the job until the last minute; procrastination is covered in chapter 4.

- Problems in the back of your mind when you are attempting to relax.

The answer to this is to write everything down. When you think of something you need to do tomorrow, or later today, make a note of it in your diary or jobs-to-do list. If several things are worrying you, write them all down. This will unload your subconscious and allow you to relax and think about *important* things.

- Deadlines coming up – uncertainty about whether they will be achieved.

Have a plan. This will usually involve breaking large tasks into chunks, ideally with milestones along the way (e.g. 'I will have read the books by Monday, planned the rough outline by Friday, and written the first draft of the report by Tuesday week. Then I'll still have five days to polish it up.' If the worst happens and your planning reveals the fact that the job cannot be done in the time, at least you now know and can take action, for example asking for help or trying to get the deadline postponed.

- Bursts of panic activity when everything hits at once.

Whilst being in the nature of many management jobs, this could be a sign that you have been procrastinating (chapter 4) and/or that you have not delegated enough (chapter 8). Ask yourself 'Could I have done that job sooner? How long in advance did I know about it?' and 'Could anyone else have done that job for me? Who would have done it if I had been away?'

- Chatty people when you are busy.

This requires assertiveness and a strategy for handling interruptions: see chapter 6.

■ Being late, and not being able to do anything about it (e.g. stuck in traffic or waiting for the photocopier).

This may be a sign that your 'hurry up' driver is making you try to squeeze too many activities into a day. Remember that good time management is not about fitting large numbers of activities into a perfectly dovetailed schedule (which will inevitably run late); rather it is about focusing on what is important and achieving the results that you want. It would be better to allow some extra time and take fill-in work with you, probably box 3 (important but not time-specific), like reading or writing.

If you have planned for delays but this one really is serious and unavoidable, then put your 'hurry up' driver aside, relax, realize that there is nothing you can do and that the world will not end by your being late. Lateness *once* is understandable, it's the habit that is insulting and unforgivable.

Finally, learn from the experience and improve your planning next time.

■ Uneasy feeling of not achieving goals at work or in life generally.

The first step is knowing what your goals are, clearly and in detail (chapter 2). The next step is making sure you spend some time on them every day. Have a plan of the actions that you need to take, and start taking them one small step at a time. Be assertive about making sure you find time to fit this box 3 time in – it is the most important part of each day.

■ Job list getting longer and longer every day – not enough time in a day to get it all done.

Don't let this put you off from writing a job list – even if it is not written down it can still get longer and it can still put stress on you. In fact the stress will probably be worse without a list in writing.

At the end of chapter 1 is a diagram showing your ten options. The only one that is not recommended is working longer hours, but if you don't take one of the other nine that is what will happen.

■ Not as physically fit as you should be.

What is your preferred type of exercise? Now look at the suggestions at the end of chapter 10 for ideas on how to make extra exercise a regular part of your life. This will really make a difference to how you feel and how much you achieve with your time. Try it for thirty days!

— Further reading

Blanchard, K. and Johnson, S. (1982) *The One Minute Manager*, Fontana (deceptively simple, and full of ideas that you can put into practice right away).

Blanchard, K. and Lorber, R. (1984) *Putting the One Minute Manager to Work*, Fontana.

Blanchard, K., Zigarmi, P. and Zigarmi, D. (1986) *Leadership and the One Minute Manager*, Fontana.

Bliss, Edwin C. (1983) *Doing It Now*, Bantam (the ultimate book on procrastination – read it today!).

Carnegie, Dale (1990) *How to Win Friends and Influence People*, Mandarin (dated in places but still a classic, and essential reading – you've probably heard of it, but have you read it?).

Covey, Stephen R. (1992) *The Seven Habits of Highly Effective People*, Simon & Schuster (a well-structured analysis of how to improve your relationships with yourself and others, made clear by many excellent stories and examples).

Fromm, Erich (1990) *To Have or To Be*, Abacus (discusses whether it is what you *have* or what you *become* that leads to a more rewarding life, and proposes changes that individuals and society can make).

Gallwey, W. Timothy (1975) *The Inner Game of Tennis*, Pan (the book is about tennis and the human mind, and considers whether competition – beating other people – or mastery – the personal quest for improvement – can lead to satisfaction, with tennis and with life in general).

Gawain, S. (1979) *Creative Visualisation*, Bantam (the ultimate book on how to get the best out of your subconscious: the instructions are simple, clear and practical, yet amazing and powerful).

Goldratt, Eli and Cox, J. (1986) *The Goal*, Creative Output (an inspiring book that shows that problems can be simplified and that good teams can solve any problem if they really want to).

Helmstetter, Shad (1986) *What to Say When You Talk to Yourself,* Thorsons (the classic book on improving your self-image by reprogramming your subconscious mind).

James, M. and Jongeward, D. (1971) *Born to Win,* Addison-Wesley (a readable and thorough guide to transactional analysis – how people interact and why – and to players of psychological games).

Jeffers, Susan (1987) *Feel the Fear and Do It Anyway,* Arrow (this book is about more than just courage; it is about the ability to control your own life and about quality of life).

Kushner, Harold (1987) *When All You've Ever Wanted Isn't Enough,* Pan (the subtitle is 'The search for a life that matters' and this book really does deliver some answers).

McCormack, Mark (1984) *What They Don't Teach You at Harvard Business School,* Fontana (full of practical advice for anyone starting out as a manager).

McGinnis, Alan Loy (1990) *The Power of Optimism,* Harper (illustrates the impact that your attitude will have on your life).

Oncken, W. (1985) *Managing Management Time: Who's Got the Monkey?,* Prentice Hall (from the originator of the monkey concept, this book is both amusing and shrewd; it deals with the politics of delegation and power within organizations, including tactics for handling difficult employees, slippery colleagues and demanding bosses).

Peck, M. Scott (1983) *The Road Less Travelled,* Hutchinson (this one book encompasses evolution, religion, the ultimate sin – read the book and find out what it is and why – and how to live a better life).

Redfield, James (1994) *The Celestine Prophecy,* Bantam (written as a novel, this book contains nine theories on how people work and how the world works, in terms of evolution and destiny).

Schwartz, David (1959) *The Magic of Thinking Big,* Aquarian (perhaps the best summary ever of how to use positive thinking in your life).

Senge, Peter (1992) *The Fifth Discipline,* Century (a fascinating book about organizations and how they learn; it includes some valuable examples of how we may feel we make choices in situations but we are in fact responding predictably to underlying structures. Only by changing these structures can we prevent the same problems being repeated).

Sheldrake, Rupert (1995) *Seven Experiments that Could Change the World*, Fourth Estate (produces real evidence that modern science cannot explain the world around us, particularly in terms of how our brains work and how they appear to be linked to each other).

Townsend, Robert (1971) *Further Up the Organisation*, Coronet (an exciting and dynamic book which explodes many of the myths of management theory).

Tracy, Brian (1985) *The Psychology of Achievement*, Nightingale Conant (tape series; the ultimate 'tape guru' – every minute contains a useful or profound idea, and this set of six tapes could not be improved on as a summary of the principles of success).

— *Index*